"HOW ARE WE EVER GOING TO PAY FOR COLLEGE?"

From stock and bond funds to a monthly savings plan, from getting the right loan to choosing a lower-cost (and perhaps better) school, Money magazine will help you get your kids through college—without going broke. Find out the answers to the questions parents ask most:

- How much is it really going to cost?
- How much financial aid can I get?
- What if the stock market goes down before my kid is ready for school?
- Is college tuition negotiable?
- Are there any special college loan programs available to my family?
- Are the most expensive schools really worth it?

Paying for Your Child's College Education

Money Magazine

Other books in the
Money ® America's Financial Advisor series:

How to Retire Young and Rich

401(k) Take Charge of Your Life

Paying for Your Child's College Education

Marguerite Smith

WARNER BOOKS

A Time Warner Company

A NOTE FROM THE PUBLISHER

This publication is designed to provide competent and reliable information regarding the subject matter covered. However, it is sold with the understanding that the author and publisher are not engaged in rendering legal, financial, or other professional advice. Laws and practices often vary from state to state and if legal or other expert assistance is required, the services of a professional should be sought. The author and publisher specifically disclaim any liability that is incurred from the use or application of the contents of this book.

Warner Books, Inc., 1271 Avenue of the Americas, New York, NY 10020

Visit our Web site at http://warnerbooks.com

 A Time Warner Company

Printed in the United States of America
First Printing: June 1996
10   9   8   7   6   5   4   3   2

Library of Congress Cataloging-in-Publication Data

Smith, Marguerite.
    Paying for your child's college education / Marguerite Smith.
      p. cm.
    Includes index.
    ISBN 0-446-67165-7
    1. Student aid—United States.   2. College costs—United States.
   3. Parents—United States—Finance, Personal.   4. Student loan
   funds—United States.   I. Title.
LB2337.4.S63   1996
378.3—dc20

Book design and composition by L&G McRee
Cover design by Bernadette Anthony
Cover illustration by Peter Huey

To Lawrence George Smith, for his continuing love, encouragement, and wisdom.

ACKNOWLEDGMENTS

Many people and organizations provided data, information, and advice that greatly enriched this book. In particular I would like to thank Jeffrey Penn, Kathleen Brouder, and all the staff at the College Board; Raymond Loewe and Connie Sexton of College Money; the Education Resources Institute; Ibbotson Associates; the National Association of College Admission Counselors; Sandy Baum, Skidmore College; Thomas C. Hayden, Oberlin College; Michael McPherson, Williams College; Michael Zuckerman, University of Pennsylvania.

For their helpful ideas and expertise, my deep appreciation to John and Maria Abbot; Debra Allee; John Barnhill, M.D.; Garfield Brown, M.D.; Todd Brown; Nicole Chebeir; Cornelia Dwyer; John and Mary Anne Grammer; Joseph Morein; Shaun O'Connell; Terence Roche Murphy; Joan and John Neary; Sam Smith.

At **MONEY** magazine, thanks to Frank Lalli, Richard Eisenberg, and Dan Green. Sincere appreciation to Joan Caplin for valuable reporting help, and to Jillian Kasky for supplying statistical information.

Finally, my special gratitude to Rick Wolff, senior editor at Warner Books.

CONTENTS

Paying for Your Child's College Education

CHAPTER ONE

Solving the College Conundrum

As a parent, you may be a little scared, and you're probably more than a little confused. Perhaps you have a newborn napping in her crib or a high school sophomore wrestling with math homework at the kitchen table—or both. Whatever the case, you're starting to think about college for your offspring. And among all the factors that go into deciding which college is best, one concern leads the list: How will you pay for it?

Good question. Families grappling with that college conundrum are facing a world turned upside down. In the mid-1970s the cost of a year at Harvard barely broke the $5,000 barrier. The big problem during those years was squeezing into a school with the rest of the baby boom. Since then consumer prices and the median income of American families with college-age children have tripled—but the cost of college has risen more than fivefold. For the privilege of enrolling in the 1995–96 class, freshmen at Harvard had to pony up an awesome $27,575. Twenty years ago the Harvard bill amounted to less than one-third of median family income; today it gobbles up more than half.

THE MIDDLE CLASS CAN'T AFFORD COLLEGE WITHOUT LOTS OF HELP

The average family can now come up with only about 30 percent of typical public college costs. The rest has to be borrowed or begged from federal or state sources.

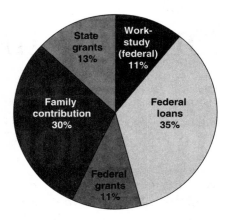

Full cost of freshman year at a typical four-year public college, 1994–95. Assumes no aid from the Federal Supplemental Education Opportunity Grant program.

Sources: MONEY magazine; City University of New York; American Association of State Colleges and Universities.

Chart 1-1

You don't have to think Ivy League to confront such punishing figures. The average family can now come up with only about 30 percent of typical public college costs. (See Chart 1-1.) The rest has to be obtained through loans and grants from the government, the institutions, or private sources. The average total cost of a year at college, both public and private, has nearly doubled during each of the past two decades. Including tuition, room, board, and mandatory fees, it's now about $6,824 at a state school and $17,630 at a private college, says the College Board, a national nonprofit educational association. A sample under-graduate annual budget, including the above costs plus books, transportation, and personal expenses, according to the College Board, jacks the necessary amounts to $9,285 and $19,762 for public and private four-year colleges respectively.

While inflation in the last decade has averaged 3.7 percent, the annual rate of increase in college expenses has been about 7 percent—higher than the rate for all other goods and services. One mildly positive note: Annual increases have eased off lately to the 6 percent range—but they still outpace inflation by a wide margin, and experts predict they are unlikely to drop much more. (See Table 1-1.)

Table 1-1

Year	College Inflation	CPI	Difference
Average	6.99%	3.57%	3.42%
1986	8.02%	1.61%	6.41%
1987	7.39%	3.90%	3.49%
1988	7.89%	4.16%	3.73%
1989	8.61%	4.99%	3.62%
1990	7.83%	4.81%	3.02%
1991	7.61%	4.45%	3.16%
1992	5.79%	3.16%	2.63%
1993	5.99%	2.78%	3.21%
1994	5.44%	2.77%	2.67%
1995	5.32%	3.04%	2.28%

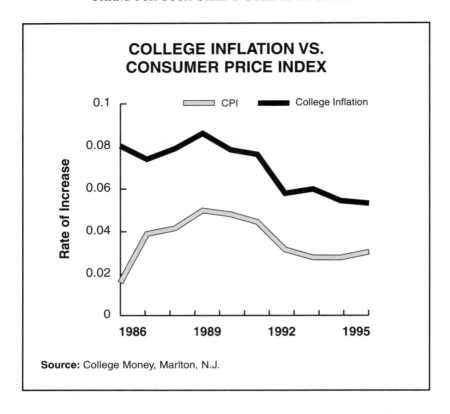

COLLEGE INFLATION VS. CONSUMER PRICE INDEX

Source: College Money, Marlton, N.J.

What's ahead: more pain. Expect a continuing onslaught of congressional proposals to limit direct federal loans and subsidies, prune grants and scholarships, trim work-study programs, and raise interest rates on future loans to parents to underwrite their kids' schooling. "It's a safe bet that Uncle Sam's largesse will diminish in years to come," says Kevin Keeley, executive director of the National Association of College Admission Counselors. "Students will cope by postponing college and working for a year or two, starting out as commuter students, and cutting costs in other ways. The struggle will teach them something about financial responsibility—but it will also infringe on the university experience."

The states, for their part, have been tightening the fiscal reins since 1992–93, when the first overall dollar cuts were imposed. "Competing priorities ranging from Medicare to prisons are taking a greater share of government budgets," says Barmak Nassirian, an analyst with the American Association of State Colleges and Universities in Washington, D.C.

Yes, we're living in an age of austerity. But don't fling up your hands yet. There's lots more wiggle room than most parents realize. Consider this: Only one out of four of those Harvard freshmen is paying the full tab. The rest are getting through on a patchwork of grants, loans, merit scholarships, and summer earnings, plus gifts from grandparents and doting uncles. Nationwide, loans have grown from being the exception to being the norm: more than 50 percent of students graduating from four-year colleges are in debt, according to the American Council on Education.

Your family may indeed have to borrow, postpone the boat, the new car, the Caribbean cruise. But the chances are excellent that you and your high schooler, with help from his or her college of choice, can piece together a financial lifeboat to carry him or her to that golden bachelor's degree. Brains count, but persistence and ingenuity count most.

As a first step though, families that can save for their children's college education should do so. Kathleen Brouder, director of the Information Services of the College Scholarship Service, the financial arm of the College Board, describes college as a "shared responsibility," where the government, the school, families, and students must play their part. "Parents should weigh the value of a college education for their children and plan ahead," Brouder advises. "Prudent saving and some sacrifices along the way will pay off for children in the long run."

A common misperception is that it's unwise to save for college because it will disqualify you in the competition for financial aid. It's true that much of the available aid is need based, and people with assets have a greater capacity to pay than those with similar incomes but no financial reserves. Many assets, however, including 401(k)s and other retirement accounts, have no effect on the amount of federal aid for which your child will qualify, and others have only a small impact. Uncle Sam ignores any assets for families with incomes below $50,000. Ultimately you aren't severely penalized for thrift: an extra $1,000 of savings will increase the contribution you are expected to make by a maximum of $56.

Having the savings, however, will clearly make college much easier for you and your youngster. The funds may even help your John or Jane win admission, as more colleges, particularly private schools, are taking into account a student's ability to pay when deciding whom to admit. A 1995 survey by the National Association of College Admission Counselors found that 26 percent of schools consider the ability to pay when they are making admissions decisions. Financial need can definitely be a strike against a student when the school is filling the last few slots in an entering class.

In drawing up a college game plan, be prepared to rethink your ideas about borrowing. A 1995 study by the Education Resources Institute, "College Debt and the American Family," reports that borrowing to pay for college has soared in recent years, with federal loan programs disbursing more in the last four years than in their first 20. In 1984 students and parents borrowed $7.9 billion for higher education. By the end of 1994 that figure had grown to $23.1 billion, with more than half of that increase coming in the past two years. The report predicts that total borrowing will increase to almost $50 billion by the year 2000, from $24 billion in 1995. One reason: The cost of public and private colleges (for tuition, fees, and room and board) has been outstripping the growth in disposable personal income by two or three percentage points year in, year out. (See Chart 1-2.)

Don't let these numbers scare you away, however, for there's a positive payoff ahead. "The earnings premium for people with higher skills and education has increased dramatically since the late 1970s," says Isabel Sawhill, senior fellow at the Urban Institute in Washington, D.C. According to the U.S. Census Bureau, in 1993 the median income for a college graduate was

6

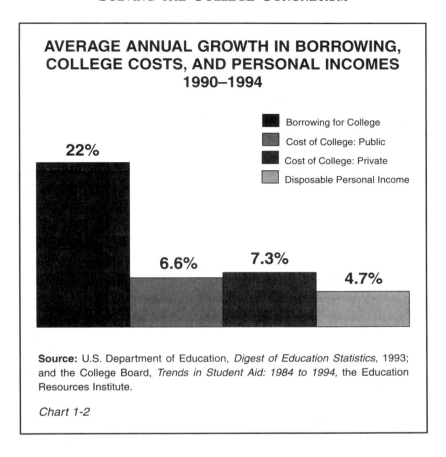

AVERAGE ANNUAL GROWTH IN BORROWING, COLLEGE COSTS, AND PERSONAL INCOMES 1990–1994

■ Borrowing for College
■ Cost of College: Public
■ Cost of College: Private
■ Disposable Personal Income

22%

6.6%   7.3%

4.7%

Source: U.S. Department of Education, *Digest of Education Statistics,* 1993; and the College Board, *Trends in Student Aid: 1984 to 1994,* the Education Resources Institute.

Chart 1-2

$27,470, about 90 percent higher than for a worker with only a high school diploma. Twenty years ago the difference was only 50 percent. Today's median for someone with a master's: $35,848; with a doctorate: $47,970.

"Because college graduates have dramatically higher earnings, borrowing for college is more like borrowing to start a promising company than like taking out a vacation loan," says Raymond Loewe, president of College Money, a financial-planning firm in Marlton, N.J. Indeed, the average new car costs about as much as the average year at a private college—and many people replace those wheels every few years. Not true with college: four years and it's typically over. "You don't need to shell out forever," Loewe points out. "It's a short-term problem."

In some cases, he advises, it's better to borrow temporarily than to invade financial assets. If you can earn 9 percent on your investments and borrow at a lower rate, let your money continue to grow. When senior year comes around, use your profits to pay off the loans.

Fortunately, higher education is unlike medical care (that other potential budget buster) in that it follows a predictable schedule and lasts for a limited period—which makes it easy to plan for. This book will help you and your child tilt the affordability odds in your favor, whether you have two months, two years, or two decades before the first tuition bill arrives. In the next two chapters we'll propose a raft of ideas about laying the groundwork—the financial twists and turns of zeroing in on which kind of college might provide the right education for your child and give good value as well. In Chapters 4 and 5 you'll learn how to build your college fund, using sophisticated strategies that will work whether your child is six or 16. Starting in Chapter 6, you'll get keys to help you unlock the financial aid coffers. It's a system that can be maddeningly complex, yet surprisingly generous to those who master its intricacies. Finally we'll show you how to borrow wisely, if that's necessary to bridge the gap.

"The Endpaper" finishes with candid advice from parents who have been through the process, on how to limit emotional and financial costs. They speak out on subjects ranging from socks (no kidding) to stocks. The appendix names 100 colleges that have proven over the years that you can get a topflight education without paying killer prices.

For now, drop the idea that price is the key determinant. Start thinking about what education means to you and your child and what kind of college will provide it. Rest easy: you're not searching for a needle in a haystack. Don't feel you must unearth the one right school from the 2,149 four-year colleges out there. For most youngsters there are dozens of good choices. When you and your child set the basic parameters, so you have a vision of what you're aiming for, the following chapters will show you how to get there with minimal financial pain.

- Save steadily, starting as early as possible. The stash won't squelch your eligibility for financial aid, and it may help your child's admission chances, especially at private colleges. In addition, those four years will be far less of a strain for you and your student.
- Be prepared for you and your child to borrow if necessary. A college degree may cost as much as a house—and you didn't flinch from taking out a mortgage, did you? There are still some attractive education loans out there.
- Keep your eyes on the prize. People who are better educated earn better incomes—and often have richer, more interesting lives. When you endow your child with a college education, you'll have the satisfaction of knowing that you have given him or her an invaluable tool to maximize his or her full potential.

CHAPTER TWO

What Will College Really Cost Me?

There is an enormous and crucial difference between the official cost of a college education and the cost of that college education to *you*. In this chapter we will explore two trends that help explain that difference: college costs that continue to rise faster than inflation, and a basic upheaval taking place in college admissions and financial aid giving. We'll show you how you can use the second to help offset the first.

By now you probably have some notion of the kind of college—two- or four-year, public or private, close to home or a continent away—for which your youngster is aiming. (Alternatively, you know the kind of place that you are dreaming of for him or her, if first grade is closer than freshman year.) And if you are considering specific institutions it's easy enough to find the posted sticker price. What's missing, though, is a sense of what it will ultimately cost you—especially if those freshman bells will be pealing some years hence.

If you think your goal will keep getting more expensive, you are, of course, right. Evidence: **MONEY** magazine's 1994 *College Guide* listed a mere six schools that charged more than $25,000 for one year's tuition, fees, and room and board. (The priciest then was Brandeis University at $26,130, followed by Barnard, MIT, Hampshire College, Yale, and Bard College at $25,044.) The 1996 *Guide* lists fully 69 institutions that exceed the $25,000 benchmark. (Sarah Lawrence tops the list, at $28,582.)

So that you can see how the trend of rising costs will play out, we've included here basic financial projections for colleges at three price levels for freshmen entering in 1996 to 2006. We also spell out the approximate monthly savings required to meet those costs, assuming they are rising about 6.5 percent a year (or, if you've just struck the lottery, the lump sum you could invest today to fund those future college years). Seeing these projected figures in black and white could give a sharp kick to your savings motivations.

DOLLARS FOR YOUR SCHOLAR

The following three tables estimate the total costs of college, including tuition, room and board, fees, books, travel, and other miscellaneous costs that parents report. We assume a 7 percent after-tax growth on your savings, and that college costs will rise about 6.5 percent per year. Cost categories range from one (for in-state residents attending a state school) to three (for the Ivy league elite). Number two is the medium range for private schools.

Table 2-1

PROJECTED FRESHMAN YEAR	PROJECTED FRESHMAN COST	PROJECTED SOPHOMORE COST	PROJECTED JUNIOR COST	PROJECTED SENIOR COST	PROJECTED FOUR YEAR COST	LUMP SUM REQ. TODAY	APPROX. MO. SAVINGS REQ.
1996	$12,100	$12,900	$13,700	$14,600	$53,300	$44,897	$1,069
1997	$12,900	$13,700	$14,600	$15,500	$56,700	$44,640	$879
1998	$13,700	$14,600	$15,500	$16,600	$60,400	$44,434	$753
1999	$14,600	$15,500	$16,600	$17,800	$64,500	$44,336	$665
2000	$15,500	$16,600	$17,800	$19,000	$68,900	$44,256	$600
2001	$16,600	$17,800	$19,000	$20,300	$73,700	$44,246	$550
2002	$17,800	$19,000	$20,300	$21,700	$78,800	$44,216	$510
2003	$19,000	$20,300	$21,700	$23,200	$84,200	$44,153	$478
2004	$20,300	$21,700	$23,200	$24,800	$90,000	$44,107	$451
2005	$21,700	$23,200	$24,800	$26,500	$96,200	$44,061	$428
2006	$23,200	$24,800	$26,500	$28,400	$102,900	$44,044	$410
2007	$24,800	$26,500	$28,400	$30,400	$110,100	$44,040	$394
2008	$26,500	$28,400	$30,400	$32,500	$117,800	$44,038	$380
2009	$28,400	$30,400	$32,500	$34,600	$126,100	$44,058	$368
2010	$30,400	$32,500	$34,800	$37,200	$134,900	$44,050	$357
2011	$32,500	$34,600	$37,200	$39,800	$144,300	$44,037	$348
2012	$34,600	$37,200	$39,800	$42,600	$154,400	$44,037	$339
2013	$37,200	$39,800	$42,600	$45,600	$165,200	$44,033	$332
2014	$39,800	$42,600	$45,600	$48,800	$176,800	$44,041	$326
2015	$42,600	$45,600	$48,800	$52,200	$189,200	$44,048	$320
2016	$45,600	$48,800	$52,200	$55,900	$202,500	$44,060	$314

Table 2-2

PROJECTED FRESHMAN YEAR	PROJECTED FRESHMAN COST	PROJECTED SOPHOMORE COST	PROJECTED JUNIOR COST	PROJECTED SENIOR COST	PROJECTED FOUR YEAR COST	LUMP SUM REQ. TODAY	APPROX. MO. SAVINGS REQ.
1996	$23,800	$25,300	$26,900	$28,600	$104,600	$88,118	$2,098
1997	$25,300	$26,900	$28,600	$30,500	$111,300	$87,621	$1,725
1998	$26,900	$28,600	$30,500	$32,600	$118,600	$87,246	$1,479
1999	$28,600	$30,500	$32,600	$34,900	$126,600	$87,022	$1,306
2000	$30,500	$32,600	$34,900	$37,300	$135,300	$86,912	$1,178
2001	$32,600	$34,900	$37,300	$39,900	$144,700	$86,869	$1,080
2002	$34,900	$37,300	$39,900	$42,700	$154,800	$86,852	$1,003

PROJECTED FRESHMAN YEAR	PROJECTED FRESHMAN COST	PROJECTED SOPHOMORE COST	PROJECTED JUNIOR COST	PROJECTED SENIOR COST	PROJECTED FOUR YEAR COST	LUMP SUM REQ. TODAY	APPROX. MO. SAVINGS REQ.
2003	$37,300	$39,900	$42,700	$45,700	$165,600	$86,830	$940
2004	$39,900	$42,700	$45,700	$48,900	$177,200	$86,833	$888
2005	$42,700	$45,700	$48,900	$52,300	$189,600	$86,833	$844
2006	$45,700	$48,900	$52,300	$56,000	$202,900	$86,844	$808
2007	$48,900	$52,300	$56,000	$59,900	$217,100	$86,843	$776
2008	$52,300	$56,000	$59,900	$64,100	$232,300	$86,844	$749
2009	$56,000	$59,900	$64,100	$68,600	$248,600	$86,858	$725
2010	$59,900	$64,100	$68,600	$73,400	$266,000	$86,857	$704
2011	$64,100	$68,600	$73,400	$78,500	$264,600	$86,852	$666
2012	$68,600	$73,400	$78,500	$84,000	$304,500	$86,847	$669
2013	$73,400	$78,500	$84,000	$89,900	$325,800	$86,842	$655
2014	$78,500	$84,000	$89,900	$96,200	$348,600	$86,839	$642
2015	$84,000	$89,900	$96,200	$102,900	$373,000	$86,839	$630
2016	$89,900	$96,200	$102,900	$110,100	$399,100	$86,838	$620

Table 2-3

PROJECTED FRESHMAN YEAR	PROJECTED FRESHMAN COST	PROJECTED SOPHOMORE COST	PROJECTED JUNIOR COST	PROJECTED SENIOR COST	PROJECTED FOUR YEAR COST	LUMP SUM REQ. TODAY	APPROX. MO. SAVINGS REQ.
1996	$29,800	$31,700	$33,800	$36,000	$131,300	$110,594	$2,633
1997	$31,700	$33,800	$36,000	$38,300	$139,800	$110,050	$2,166
1998	$33,800	$36,000	$38,300	$41,000	$149,100	$109,682	$1,859
1999	$36,000	$38,300	$41,000	$43,900	$159,200	$109,430	$1,642
2000	$38,300	$41,000	$43,900	$47,000	$170,200	$109,321	$1,482
2001	$41,000	$43,900	$47,000	$50,300	$182,200	$109,373	$1,360
2002	$43,900	$47,000	$50,300	$53,800	$195,000	$109,402	$1,263
2003	$47,000	$50,300	$53,800	$57,600	$208,700	$109,429	$1,184
2004	$50,300	$53,800	$57,600	$61,600	$223,300	$109,426	$1,119
2005	$53,800	$57,600	$61,600	$65,900	$238,900	$109,412	$1,064
2006	$57,600	$61,600	$65,900	$70,500	$255,600	$109,404	$1,017
2007	$61,600	$65,900	$70,500	$75,400	$273,400	$109,367	$977
2008	$65,900	$70,500	$75,400	$80,700	$292,500	$109,352	$943

Projected Freshman Year	Projected Freshman Cost	Projected Sophomore Cost	Projected Junior Cost	Projected Senior Cost	Projected Four Year Cost	Lump Sum Req. Today	Approx. Mo. Savings Req.
2009	$70,500	$75,400	$80,700	$86,300	$312,900	$109,326	$913
2010	$75,400	$80,700	$86,300	$92,300	$334,700	$109,293	$886
2011	$80,700	$86,300	$92,300	$98,800	$358,100	$109,284	$863
2012	$86,300	$92,300	$98,800	$105,700	$383,100	$109,263	$842
2013	$92,300	$98,800	$105,700	$113,100	$409,900	$109,257	$824
2014	$98,800	$105,700	$113,100	$121,000	$438,600	$109,260	$808
2015	$105,700	$113,100	$121,000	$129,500	$469,300	$109,259	$793
2016	$113,100	$121,000	$129,500	$138,600	$502,200	$109,269	$780

Prepared by College Money, Marlton, N.J.

Enough of numbing numbers. The good news is that many colleges are changing some time-hallowed admissions policies in ways that can benefit the parent who does save and the student who does study. The help comes in two ways: you might be able to get discounted tuition if you need it; if you don't require financial assistance, your child may qualify for a more competitive college than might have been possible in earlier years.

The basic reason for these changes is that there is a supply/demand imbalance. America's college-age population has declined 13.5 percent since 1975 to 14 million today. This has left hundreds of student-hungry schools more willing than ever to boost their financial aid offers by cutting deals with parents and their children. (See Table 2-4, for a list of the nation's top 10 college discounters.) "I've heard financial aid officers refer to the weeks after the offer letters go out as 'Let's make a deal' time," says Michael McPherson, co-director of the Williams College Project on the Economics of Higher Education.

Table 2-4

TOP 10 COLLEGE GIFT GIVERS

These colleges award the largest percentage of funds in scholarships, grants, and other student subsidies. Listed are each school's average gift aid per student and the percentage of total costs that it covers.

College	Total Cost	Gift Aid	% of Cost
Pikeville College (Ky.)	$9,000	$6,386	71
Wiley College (Texas)	7,026	4,324	62
Alcorn State U. (Miss.)	6,737	3,261	48
Sweet Briar College (Va.)	21,500	9,444	44
Monmouth College (Ill.)	17,860	7,579	42
Wabash College (Ind.)	18,355	7,736	42
Bennington College (Vt.)	25,800	10,236	40
Benedict College (S.C.)	9,490	3,385	36
Brewton-Parker College (Ga.)	7,470	2,716	36
Missouri Valley College	14,550	5,202	36

Source: MONEY magazine.

Although the trends are in your favor, don't assume you can just waltz into a college's financial aid office and demand more money. Only families that know how to negotiate shrewdly can expect to emerge with an enriched aid package. The basic hitch: You'll need something to negotiate with. And you'll need a working acquaintance with the latest college financial aid practices: preferential packaging, gapping, admit/deny policies, and that hot-button phrase, "need-blind admissions." (We'll explain these terms later in the chapter.) For the moment it's enough to know that preferential packaging is your goal, gapping and admit/deny are what to avoid, and that need-blind admissions is an endangered species. When you learn how these work, they can serve as tools to advance your cause of getting generous aid from institutions so you don't have to carry the entire formidable financial burden yourself.

If you still have qualms about the dollars required to attain your child's degree, remember that tuition isn't the only item that inflates over time. Your income will also, sometimes at rates that beat inflation. Even better, if you instill in your child the idea that knowledge adds more to the quality of life than mere cash, that can also ease your obligation. If your kid really likes learning, colleges will seek him or her out with merit aid in hand.

College Admissions: Savings vs. SATs

Start with this premise: Higher education is splitting into two camps—the haves and the have-nots. The first group includes the Ivies, Stanford, California Institute of Technology, and similar schools that can charge almost any amount and still command the cream of the student crop. "Their budgets are expanding, they're enriching their curricula, their residence halls stay spruced up," says Williams's Michael McPherson. "But hundreds of other private schools are under enormous strain. They have to emulate these models, without the same endowment resources, which compels them to charge high tuitions."

At the same time, many small private colleges and universities—even distinguished ones like Oberlin and Skidmore—are losing candidates to state-subsidized universities. Middle-class parents rebel at their relatively high prices and end up shipping off their kids to good old affordable—and often academically respectable—State U.

This middle-class flight has, in effect, changed financial aid into a form of selective price discounting at many of the second-tier liberal arts colleges and universities. This group may offer discounted tuitions (in the form of grants, though no money changes hands) to students who are unwilling to pay full freight. They may be even more generous to desirable students whose enrollments can enhance the school's reputation—the practice referred to earlier as **preferential packaging.** Merit-based aid—which rewards excellence over financial need—has been growing far more quickly than need-based aid in recent years, according to a study by McPherson and economist Morton Schapiro of the University of Southern California, Los Angeles.

Twenty years ago schools viewed aid money as a kind of charity operation run on the side. Now, says McPherson, "schools look at financial aid as a strategic instrument for shaping the quality of the entering class." Whatever accomplishments the college values can be rewarded, be it high SAT scores, musical talent, or the ability to ace the 100-meter dash. Example: McPherson's son Steven got a brochure from a college saying, in effect, "Look up your SAT scores in column A, then find the amount of your scholarship in column B." (Steven, now a sophomore, went elsewhere, without a merit scholarship.)

Over the years, American colleges have come to be known as **need-blind,** which means they admit candidates on the basis of academic and personal accomplishments, ignoring financial need as a consideration in selecting students. Many parents assume, as a corollary, that need-blind institutions also meet an applicant's full financial need, making it possible for students who are admitted to the college to actually attend the school. In fact, only a precious handful of institutions can meet full demonstrated need with reasonable aid packages. Some academicians maintain that no more than 20 schools nationwide continue a pure need-blind policy. "No one knows how to verify that figure, but everyone believes it," says Thomas C. Hayden, vice president for admissions and financial aid at Oberlin College. "The others are trying very hard to meet students' financial need, but many of them are forced to gap behind the scenes."

Gapping, a relatively new practice, occurs when an admitted student is awarded a financial aid package that meets less than his or her full demonstrated need. The school awards what it can and hopes that a rich grandparent or other source will emerge to bridge the financial gap. More draconian is **admit/deny,** a strategy in which all students are admitted through a need-blind process, but some portion of the admitted students who demonstrate need are denied financial aid.

According to a 1994 study by the National Association of College Admission Counselors, 65 percent of college and universities practice gapping, 54 percent use preferential packaging, and 21 percent employ admit/deny policies. Among public schools that have adopted preferential packaging, the top priority was to attract students of desirable ethnicity; academic merit ranked second. The priorities of the private schools were reversed, with academic merit leading the list.

What this means for parents like you is that thrift is likely to pay off both directly and indirectly. Money in the bank will surely help you and your child more comfortably survive those four expensive years—but it may also make the school more likely to admit your scholar.

The growing trend toward merit aid tilts the admissions seesaw toward middle- and upper-income families. Applicants most likely to benefit are the excellent students (who may get grants even if they don't need the money) and academically marginal students from families that can afford to pay the full tab. "I'm seeing a definite trend among my senior acceptances," says Todd Brown, a science teacher at Wooster, a private secondary school in Danbury, Conn. "Those who are able to pay full tuition are getting into colleges that were, in the past, out of their league academically. This has provided opportunities at my school, as there's a good deal of wealth here in Fairfield County."

Your next move is to amass a list of 20 or so colleges that you and your child agree will suit his or her interests and talents. Then you must tackle some preliminary financial evaluations, and we'll show you how to do just that.

- Bone up on the latest college financial aid practices, particularly preferential packaging, to help your child present the best possible case on his or her application.
- Encourage your child to achieve good grades and seriously develop one or two extracurricular interests. Colleges will often grant more merit money to a brain—or to an athlete, musician or actor—if they want to round out their freshman class in a specific direction.

CHAPTER THREE

Finding Your Best College Buys

Helping your child hunt for the right college is a delicate ritual of passage. The child may make the final choice, but as a parent you must keep the search on course to be sure that the school suits the young applicant's interests and talents. Then you can feel confident that you aren't wasting the tens of thousands of dollars that degree may be costing you. (To see how sharp the bite can get, consult Table 3-1, which lists the 25 schools with the highest charges for tuition, fees, and room and board.) Even as costs continue to escalate, in many places faculties are shrinking, curriculums are narrowing, and students are taking longer to graduate. Classrooms are crowded, campuses shabbier.

Table 3-1

LUXURY DEGREES:
SCHOOLS WITH THE HIGHEST CHARGES FOR
TUITION, FEES, AND ROOM AND BOARD

Sarah Lawrence College (N.Y.)	$28,582
Hampshire College (Mass.)	28,275
Barnard College (N.Y.)	27,844
Massachusetts Institute of Technology	27,762
Princeton University (N.J.)	27,756
Brandeis University (Mass.)	27,685
Yale University (Conn.)	27,630
Harvard University (Mass.)	27,575
Bard College (N.Y.)	27,499
University of Chicago (Ill.)	27,451
Pomona College (Calif.)	27,300
New York University	27,300
Middlebury College (Vt.)	27,190
Stanford University (Calif.)	27,141
Columbia University (N.Y.)	27,126
University of Pennsylvania	27,080
Swarthmore College (Pa.)	27,066
Brown University (R.I.)	27,054
Tufts University (Mass.)	27,033
Reed College (Ore.)	27,010
Bryn Mawr College (Pa.)	26,895
Cornell University (N.Y.)	26,828
Boston University (Mass.)	26,800
Trinity College (Conn.)	26,795
Williams College (Mass.)	26,780

Source: MONEY magazine.

These factors make it more necessary than ever to uncover the institutions that will meet your child's needs. You'll need to check out a school's financial health as well as its academic and social character. You don't know if the college Jane enters as a freshman will be the same place when she's a graduating senior. Maybe the linguistics department will vanish just as she's decided to major in that area. The more effort you and your offspring put into investigating schools now, the happier you're both likelier to be with the final choice.

Don't expect this to be an easy task, however. "It's very hard to get real information about the quality of a college," says Michael McPherson, co-director of the Williams College Project on the Economics of Higher Education.

Colleges aren't candid when they're competing for students. As the struggle for applicants has heated up, many schools have done their best to camouflage imperfections. Their admissions materials often look like glossy sales brochures, their videos are close cousins to TV commercials. Understandably, perhaps, college marketing tends to focus on lifestyle, not education. Sunflower State wants your child to see it as a haven where romance and friendship flourish. It's not likely to volunteer to Johnny that overflow students listen to lectures on TV monitors, that he'll have to learn calculus from a teaching assistant whose native tongue is Farsi, or that a campus housing shortage might force him to live in a trailer.

As a college shopper, don't be overly trusting. Get answers to tough questions, rather than simply being in awe of the manicured lawns or the football team's record. Williams's Michael McPherson offers the following suggestions to help parents and children gain a sense of what the daily college experience will be like:

• On the *academic* side, be aware that every college claims to be a center of academic excellence—yet schools vary more in that area than in anything else. Check out the claim by seeing how full the library is on a weekday evening. At 10:30 on a Wednesday night, is the dorm filled with people studying, or is it party time?

Investigate class sizes. The view book will invariably have a photograph of a faculty member imparting knowledge or discussing ideas with a dozen or so students in a small room. Ask how many students are in the core classes. If Biology 1 has 800 students, your daughter who's premed should be prepared to cope with that in advance. In the same vein, find out what percentage of freshman courses are taught by members of the faculty rather than by teaching assistants.

If your child's interests are relatively specialized, can the school continue to meet his or her needs? Some schools can be far more accommodating (and have broader course offerings) than others. Joan Neary of Tesuque, New Mex., recalls that as a Vassar undergraduate her son John signed up for a narrowly focused art course—in which he turned out to be the sole enrollee. "And Vassar gave him the class!" she marvels, still grateful.

Your child may not luck into an individual tutorial as young Neary did, but you should test the school's involvement with undergraduate education. Pick the subject your child is likely to major in, then phone the chairman of the department. "Many of them won't return your call," says McPherson, "which may indicate a lack of concern about the quality of the undergraduate experience." If the chairman or a colleague does phone you back, inquire about the content of the introductory course in the subject. "You'd be surprised at how many of them won't know," McPherson laments. If large lecture courses predominate in the department, find out how much training (if any) is given to teaching assistants, especially in grading.

• To learn about the *social* side, have your child spend one or two nights in a residence house. College brochures will always present the dorms as exciting living/learning environments. Some are, but some are so exciting that they're right out of *Animal House*. Other places, the dorms empty out on weekends and the kid who's left behind may be miserable.

The essential question to resolve is this: Is the social life reasonably varied, or is there a single norm to which students are under pressure to conform? This isn't much of a worry at a large state university. At the University of Wisconsin, for instance, your daughter can probably find 10 other kids who are as crazy about Hungarian stick dancing as she is. But social homogeneity can be a serious issue at a small school. "If the large majority of students stay drunk from Thursday night through Saturday," says McPherson, "the student who's not a party animal may end up sitting alone in her room."

Similarly, if it's a fraternity school, find out if the Greeks dominate social life or if they are just one of many players. At some schools eating clubs may be a divisive element among undergraduates. "My daughter looked at a college where 80 percent of the women belonged to one of three eating clubs," says Cornelia Dwyer, of Atlanta, Ga. "That meant that only 20 percent of upper-class women were eating in the dining hall, and we didn't like that." Such factors can strongly color your child's daily college experience.

If you belong to a minority group, visit the dining hall at lunchtime and observe whether black, Hispanic, Asian, and white students are mixed around the room or sit apart in separate clumps. Take time to do a little shopping nearby, and gauge your reception by local merchants. You may want to subscribe to the school newspaper. If race relations are tense, you'll soon find out. You want to eliminate any college where your child may encounter entrenched racial hostility or isolation.

Overnight dorm visits are the single best way to get a sense of the school's social climate—and they allow the future undergraduate a chance for reality testing in multiple areas. "We found that the most trivial things could have unexpected impact," says a father from Basking Ridge, N.J., who shepherded two sons on college jaunts. "For example, one of my sons dropped a school off his list when the student whose room he had shared overnight casually mentioned that the dorm's resident assistant was gay. My other son fell in love with the school where his overnight dorm stay included a tour of the local bars." These may not be *your* dream criteria, but it's best that your child should learn the facts of daily life early on and filter them into his decision making.

By now you may be wondering, how do you narrow the universe of colleges and universities to a manageable number to investigate seriously? Martin Nemko, who runs a private college counseling service in Oakland, Calif., maintains that five basic questions can help you and your child reduce the list to 20 or so schools in about half an hour:

1. *Two-year vs. four-year schools.* Choosing four years reduces the list about 35 percent to 2,149 schools, in 20 seconds.

2. *Public or private.* This is often a cost issue, unless you're expecting to qualify for a lot of financial aid or are so rich that it doesn't matter. Of course, you may have family ties to the local university, or your child may want to go because his friends are heading there, so sentiment can also play a part.

3. *Proximity to home.* Around 80 percent of students stay within 200 miles of home. So if your child chooses to remain in that radius, and you live in a metro area and not the wilds of Wyoming, that could leave you with a selection of 50 to 200 schools. If your offspring is bent on a single-sex school, that will shorten the list even further.

4. *Selectivity.* This will take longer, for it requires some soul-searching by you and your offspring. Is Johnny content to be a lesser light among the future stars of his generation? Or will it be better for his personal development to shine in the second tier? Together, try to thrash out a preliminary answer.

5. *Size.* Young Jane may think smaller is better, but will she outgrow that intimate rural college by her junior year? Or will she disappear among the thousands of students in a giant state uni-

versity? The two of you will have to look ahead, or perhaps make some visits, to try to arrive at the truth.

By now you should have whittled the list to around 20 names. Eventually most kids should apply to about five or six. Going through the elimination process means that you and your off-spring have to decide which factors are likely to maximize his or her happiness and success—which means identifying academic and social strengths and weaknesses. "Choosing a college obliges a lot of introspection," says University of Pennsylvania American history professor Michael Zuckerman. "Does a kid from an affluent suburb where it's fairly homogeneous want more of the same in college or something radically different? Does a working-class kid want to try an elite school where most of the students are much richer than she is?"

For your child, it boils down to discovering who he is—and is that okay? Or would he rather be someone different? Maybe a whole lot different? "It's a time for taking stock," concludes Zuckerman, the father of two college graduates, a college sophomore, and two grade-schoolers.

When you've worked your way through the process together, you and your son or daughter will be able to evaluate, in a focused way, the schools you visit. Jane or John will have ideas about what questions to ask. You won't end up aimlessly wandering the grounds, noting if the grass is green and the kids seem friendly.

While your child is weeding out her list, making final decisions about which half dozen colleges will be the honored recipients of her applications, you have homework of your own to do. Find out how much cash each of the colleges under serious consideration has to spread around to entering freshmen. You can obtain this information by asking college financial aid offices directly for the average percentage of costs covered by their aid packages and what portion of aid is given in loans (that have to be repaid) rather than grants (which don't).

Alternatively, consult college directories, available in libraries and high school counseling offices, which contain data about financial aid at virtually all accredited institutions. For now, look at Table 3-2 for the names of schools that give the most merit-based financial aid for academic and other accomplishments, and at Table 3-3 for schools that provide the most need-based aid from their own funds. Take a look, too, at the appendix, which lists 100 schools offering the best college buys today.

Table 3-2

AID FOR THE AFFLUENT: SCHOOLS THAT HAND OUT THE BIGGEST AVERAGE MERIT-BASED SCHOLARSHIPS

Buena Vista College (Iowa)	$4,447
Alma College (Mich.)	3,960
Converse College (S.C.)	3,925
Wabash College (Ind.)	3,757
Oglethorpe University (Ga.)	3,752
Delaware Valley College (Pa.)	3,609
Transylvania University (Ky.)	3,303
Washington College (Md.)	3,272
Franklin College (Ind.)	3,085
Drew University (N.J.)	2,985
Kalamazoo College (Mich.)	2,957
Culver-Stockton College (Md.)	2,836
University of Tampa (Fla.)	2,713
Missouri Valley College	2,691
Phillips University (Okla.)	2,681
Fontbonne College (Mo.)	2,668
Goucher College (Md.)	2,624
Ohio Wesleyan University	2,602

Rhodes College (Tenn.)	2,522
Muskingum College (Ohio)	2,514
Lebanon Valley College (Pa.)	2,505
West Virginia Wesleyan College	2,450
Centenary College of Louisiana	2,450
Salem-Teikyo University (W.Va.)	2,445
Agnes Scott College (Ga.)	2,393

Source: MONEY magazine.

Table 3-3

GIANTS OF GENEROSITY:
SCHOOLS THAT GIVE THE BIGGEST AVERAGE GRANTS TO STUDENTS WHO QUALIFY FOR FINANCIAL AID

Middlebury College (Vt.)	$14,114
Sweet Briar College (Va.)	12,552
Amherst College (Mass.)	12,124
Bryn Mawr College (Pa.)	11,826
Swarthmore College (Pa.)	11,681
Reed College (Ore.)	11,471
Bennington College (Vt.)	11,393
Barnard College (N.Y.)	11,053
Pomona College (Calif.)	10,717
Connecticut College	10,636
Brandeis University (Mass.)	10,591
Union College (N.Y.)	10,513
Colgate University (N.Y.)	10,508
Stanford University (Calif.)	10,405
Vassar College (N.Y.)	10,379

Smith College (Mass.)	10,098
Sarah Lawrence College (N.Y.)	10,063
Hampshire College (Mass.)	10,017
Denison University (Ohio)	9,955
Colby College (Maine)	9,929
Massachusetts Institute of Technology	9,838
Trinity College (Conn.)	9,806
Haverford College (Pa.)	9,780
Harvard University (Mass.)	9,744
Menlo College (Calif.)	9,740

Source: MONEY magazine.

If you're concentrating on private universities, don't be daunted by their high sticker prices. The richest institutions have millions of dollars to hand out, so they may actually be cheaper than less glamorous names. Many high-ticket private schools, including Stanford, Princeton, and the University of Chicago, award financial aid to at least half of their incoming freshmen.

If your student is aiming not for these superstars, but for the lesser lights of academia, you may do well to investigate the institutions' fiscal strength. In these rocky financial times, some small, private institutions are pruning course offerings, shedding services, and even shutting their doors altogether. In May 1995 Upsala College in East Orange, N.J., founded in 1893, closed permanently; three classes of undergraduates were forced to transfer to other schools, and many students lost credits in the process.

Symptoms of this kind of financial malaise invariably appear years before the final demise, but you have to know what signals to look for. One vital sign of financial health in a private college is the percentage of its endowment that goes to pay current expenses. (You can ask at the office of the treasurer.) A figure above 6 percent could indicate weakness.

Also ask if the college has recently closed any departments or trimmed services—or plans to do so. If the answers aren't forthcoming, ask an editor on the college newspaper whether the school has had difficulty retaining key administrators and faculty members. If the universities' major players are bailing out, you may not want to have your child sign on. As a final check, ask the school's development office about alumni financial support. If fewer than half of the old grads contribute annually to their alma mater, that could be a fiscal warning sign.

Among state universities, the trend is away from the generous help offered in the past. State legislators are becoming increasingly tight-fisted with funding, though annual tuition hikes no longer run at 11 percent and 14 percent, as they did in the early 1980s. Still, state-supported universities in California, New York, Maine, and Massachusetts have been laying off faculty or prodding them into early retirement. Even where budget problems are less dire, students could face curtailed course offerings, increasingly crowded classrooms, shorter library hours, and scruffier campuses.

Budget cuts notwithstanding, if your son or daughter is a middle-of-the-pack student, the in-state public colleges and universities often remain the best choice for a reasonably priced higher education. And if the public schools in your state are your child's target group, you'll certainly learn of budgetary woes or faculty cuts through your local newspapers.

If, however, your child prefers to cross state lines, you might encourage him or her to concentrate on the richest of the public institutions. The University of Texas system boasts an endowment of $4.5 billion, and tuitions are correspondingly low. If your high schooler is considering out-of-state schools that are meagerly endowed, then learn all you can about the state's fiscal condition. Call the office of higher education, usually located in the state capital, and ask if the institution you're interested in has recently eliminated any areas of study or cut back services or has plans to do so.

Finally, relax and remember that the college decision is not the equivalent of finding a contact lens in a bucket of marbles. "Most students would be happy at most of the schools that they think they'd be interested in," says Penn's Zuckerman. "And they would all be a lot happier if they weren't so caught up in making the perfect choice." While tension is inevitable during the course of choosing a college, encourage your child to look at the grander picture: "There aren't too many moments in life when we Americans are invited to stop and try to figure ourselves out," says Zuckerman. "This is one of the most serious, most challenging, and, at the same time, most fun." Advice worth heeding.

- Dig for solid, factual information about the academic and social character of a college. If it's a large, research-oriented university, talk with faculty and students to estimate the amount of attention paid to undergraduate education.
- Encourage your child to spend a weeknight or two in one of the dorms. Find out if he or she feels comfortable with the prevailing social norms.
- Talk seriously with your child about the kind of college that would make a good emotional fit. Does he want a class full of kids like himself—or a group that's very different? Will she be lost in a class of thousands—or thrive on the competition? Now's the time to explore those choices.
- When your child has a list of serious contenders, investigate the current costs. At the same time, find out how much each college awards to entering freshmen in merit or need-based aid, whichever you're aiming for.
- If you have doubts about an institution's financial stability, read local newspapers or talk to college officials about your concerns. Signs of trouble to look for: layoffs of faculty and administrators; cutbacks in student services; elimination of academic departments.

CHAPTER FOUR

Proven Investment Strategies

How *are* you going to pay for baby's B.A.? That question may be responsible for the touch of gray appearing at your temples. No matter how you crunch the numbers, the answer's the same: daunting. If the prognosticators are right and tuition rises by an average 6.5 percent a year, you'll have to shell out roughly $115,000 to put your newborn infant through four years at the typical public university.

If your cherub is destined for a selective, ivy-walled campus, you're looking at a four-year bill of around $250,000. Now multiply the amounts by the number of children you have. Result: ugly figures that make many parents throw up their hands in despair.

Don't you do it. No matter what wild anxieties may disquiet your sleep, a steady investing strategy will take you to your goal. Financing your children's college education doesn't mean saving 110 percent of your salary or making young Johnny self-supporting by the age of seven.

If you start putting money aside early, you can shoulder aggressive investment risk and swing for the fences. You'll have plenty of time to slug your share of home runs and to overcome the occasional strikeout when it happens. If you're getting a late start, you can still achieve solid financial growth with a string of sturdy doubles and singles.

No matter how late you begin, or what investing strategy you adopt, you are certain to be better off than if you had saved nothing at all. Don't let the large amounts needed intimidate you into doing nothing. If you can't squirrel away the entire cost of your child's education, there are a variety of other options to explore when the time comes. Every dollar that you save now, however, is one you won't have to beg from the financial aid office of your child's college, borrow from the government or private lenders, or steal from your retirement fund.

Moreover, an early start will give your savings more years to grow through compounding. Let's say you have a two-year-old toddler and you will need about $100,000 by the time he or she turns 18. If you start saving now, you will have to set aside $225 a month at an average annual return of 10 percent to reach your goal. If you delay until your child is a 10-year-old runabout, however, you will have to put away $725 a month to achieve the same result.

To determine how much you must save, fill out the worksheet that follows. If the amount required seems painfully unattainable, start with $50 or $100 a month, then gradually increase the amounts you put aside. When your child graduates from day care into kindergarten, for instance, use any savings on nanny costs to plump up the college fund. If you pay off a car loan, put the former monthly payment into the college fund instead. Step up your contributions again when your income rises through raises or promotions.

How Much to Save Each Year for College

You can't know years in advance, of course, exactly how expensive a school your child will choose or how fast college costs will rise between now and his or her freshman year. That said, the following worksheet will give you a fair idea of the amount of money you need to set aside each year to pay the likely cost of college when the time comes.

The worksheet assumes that college costs will rise 7 percent a year (that may be a bit high, but it will give you a margin of safety). Further, the calculation assumes that your investments will earn 7 percent a year after taxes, that your child will enter college at age 18, and that you'll continue saving until he or she graduates.

Depending on how much of your child's college costs you expect to pay, you can use one of two assumptions for the figure on line 1 below: (1) the full current cost of college (either for a specific school or an average figure of $9,000 a year for public colleges, $18,800 for private ones); or (2) 50 percent of those figures, which is the current average family share after financial aid. By choosing the second assumption, for example, you'll find that if your child is three years old and headed for a state college, you'll need to set aside $1,413 annually after the first year. If she's 14 and Ivy bound, make that a punishing $8,626 a year.

1. Current one-year cost (see note above)   ———————————
2. Four-year cost in today's dollars   ———————————
   (multiply line 1 times 4)
3. Amount to invest the first year   ———————————
   (line 2 times appropriate age factor
   from column A below)
4. Amount to save at the beginning of each   ———————————
   of the following years (multiply line 3
   by the appropriate factor from column
   B below)

AGE	A	PAYMENT NUMBER	B
Newborn	.0603	2	1.040
1	.0624	3	1.082
2	.0646	4	1.125
3	.0672	5	1.170
4	.0700	6	1.217
5	.0731	7	1.265
6	.0767	8	1.316
7	.0807	9	1.369
8	.0854	10	1.423
9	.0907	11	1.480
10	.0970	12	1.540
11	.1044	13	1.601
12	.1133	14	1.665
13	.1242	15	1.732
14	.1378	16	1.801
15	.1553	17	1.873
16	.1787	18	1.948
17	.2115	19	2.026
		20	2.107
		21	2.192
		22	2.279

Source: College Money, Marlton, N.J.

Once you've determined how much you need to save, follow the investing strategies we've outlined here for the fastest growth with reasonable levels of risk. As a guide, we offer four model portfolios, designed by Ibbotson Associates, a highly respected financial research and consulting firm, for four families at different life stages (see pp.52–58). After you home in on the right mix of stocks, bonds, and cash investments for your college savings, turn to the table of 75 top-performing mutual funds on page 59 to single out the ones that match your individual needs.

The specific investments that will work best for you depend primarily on how long you have to save before your first tuition bill. For this reason we divide the following advice to parents into three parts, depending on the age of their children: the first section is meant for parents whose children are newborn to age eight; the second is for parents of grade-schoolers ages nine through 13; the third is for parents of high school students 14 and up.

If you have more than one child, set up separate portfolios, gearing the investments in each account to that child's age. Before you rush into the specific advice, however, school yourself on these universal rules, which apply to all families trying to build a college fund.

• *Seek growth with stocks.* With college prices expected to rise 6.5 to 7 percent a year, you must funnel most of your savings into equities. According to Ibbotson, since 1926 the shares of large, blue-chip companies have returned an average of 10.2 percent a year (before taxes). During the same period, stocks of small companies managed an even richer 12.4 percent return. At those rates your money would about double in seven years with blue chips and in less than six years with small stocks.

By contrast, Ibbotson's research shows that over the last 68 years, supposedly safe, sleep-tight investments such as short-term Treasury bills gained only 4.8 percent. Treasury securities of longer duration, from five to 30 years, averaged about 5 percent. Money-market investments returned an anemic 3.7 percent. "Investors have been paid a 5 percent premium to own stocks rather than cash and bonds," says Scott Lummer, a managing director of the Ibbotson Consulting Group, "and we see no reason that this premium won't continue in the future."

True, as skeptics rightfully point out, share prices periodically take drops that can be dizzying. Nonetheless, stocks haven't lost money in any eight-year holding period since World War II. Most important, the return you keep after inflation—what economists call your **real return**—is key to your ultimate success in nourishing your nest egg. As Chart 4-1 shows, only stocks have consistently trounced inflation.

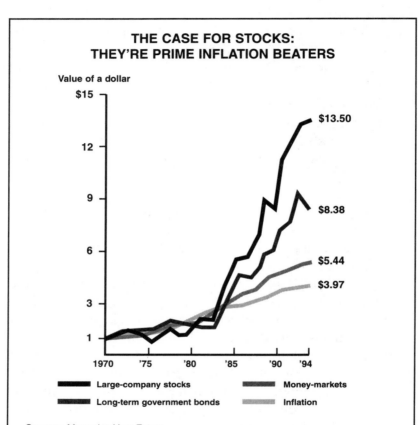

THE CASE FOR STOCKS: THEY'RE PRIME INFLATION BEATERS

Value of a dollar

- Large-company stocks
- Long-term government bonds
- Money-markets
- Inflation

Source: *Managing Your Future.*

As the graph above shows, if you had put $1 in 1970 into money-market investments, you would have had $5.44 by the end of 1994—a return of 7 percent a year. But look at inflation: to buy the goods that $1 purchased in 1970, you needed $3.97 by 1994. That means your dollar had to grow to $3.97—a return of 5.7 percent a year—just to hold its value. In other words, after subtracting inflation, money-markets earned just 1.3 percent a year.

The return you keep after inflation—what economists call your real return—is what matters over the long run. (To calculate it, just subtract the inflation rate from your investments' return.) Only stocks—which turned $1 into $13.50—have stayed far ahead of inflation. And that's why they're crucial for your college portfolio.

Chart 4-1

To brace against the periodic swings in share prices, however, you will need to adjust your child's college portfolio over time. Thus, when your child is five years or so from college, and you no longer have a lengthy period to recoup losses, you should invest somewhat more conservatively than you did in the early years. Move about 15 percent of your holdings each year out of growth stocks and into short-term bond funds, CDs, Treasury bills or notes, and other more stable investments.

• *Don't be seduced by a sales pitch for the perfect college investment.* There are no special high-yielding, ultrasafe investments that are heaven-sent for parents of college-bound kids. Banks, brokers, and others in the financial-services industry often label ordinary products—including cash-value life insurance, annuities, limited partnerships, and unit investment trusts—as ideal, risk-free vehicles to speed you to your goal. Don't be misled by glib talk or fancy marketing techniques. All these financial products are designed to achieve other financial goals—such as insuring a life or providing retirement income—and are inefficient and costly ways to pay for your child's college education. It's true that the cash value of life insurance policies typically isn't included in financial aid calculations—but Congress may close that loophole in the future. For now, sales commissions run very high, and investment returns are often mediocre.

In the end, no one-step investment solution is likely to match the returns on the diversified portfolios of plain-vanilla stocks, bonds, and cash investments described below.

• *Make investing easy with mutual funds.* This is a no-brainer. Funds offer professional management, risk-reducing diversification among different securities, and automatic reinvestment of interest, dividends, and capital-gains distributions. Another compelling attraction: Many top mutual fund companies, including Fidelity, Janus, T. Rowe Price, Twentieth Century, and Vanguard, waive or lower their usual minimum initial investment—usually $1,000 or more—if you set up an automatic investment plan to transfer a set amount from your checking or savings account to one or more funds each month or quarter. These automatic plans are an excellent, relatively painless way to save for college over time.

• *Spread your money among several funds.* Initially you may want to buy only a single stock fund. Ultimately, however, you should divvy up your money among three to five funds of different types. This will reduce your portfolio's overall risk, since dissimilar investments don't always rise or fall in tandem.

• *Be wary of putting investments in your child's name.* If you think you will have any shot at obtaining financial aid, keep most of your college savings in your name, not young Johnny's. Parental assets are still counted in the federal financial aid formula, but the accounting isn't nearly as punishing for them as it is for the future student's holdings. Kids are expected to fork over 35 percent of their assets each year to cover college costs, while parents are expected to contribute only 5.65 percent of the savings and investments held in their own names.

Perhaps you're wondering about the kiddie tax breaks that Uncle Sam still permits. True, until Johnny or Jane turns 14, the first $650 of income from assets in his or her name is tax-free and the next $650 is taxed at the child's rate, usually 15 percent. Invest just enough in your child's name to make full use of the tax break—but no more. Higher amounts are whacked at your rate, which is no break at all.

On the other hand, if your family is sufficiently prosperous that John or Jane will never qualify for aid, shifting college assets into the child's name *after* he or she turns 14 may be a smart move. At that time your offspring starts paying federal tax on all income and capital gains at his or her own rate, not yours. (An additional break: You and your spouse can each transfer up to $10,000 a year to your child without incurring a gift tax. Those funds could make excellent investment seed money, if you can afford it.) It's a sensible way to win at the tax game: your child will probably pay 15 percent, a relatively gentle nip these days and possibly less than half your rate.

Bear in mind, however, that the money *is* your child's, and you lose control over it when John or Jane comes of age, which is 18 in most states. (If the age of majority is 21 in your state, that's not a big worry, since Sunflower State will get its hands on most of the money before your child does.) Your teen could make a grand gesture by opting out and going on the road to adventure, and possibly to pot—and you would have no recourse. So if you fear that your child will heed the call of a Ferrari, exotic places, or exotic substances, keep most of the college stash in a segregated account of your own. You and your spouse will have to make this judgment call.

• *Don't neglect your retirement.* If you really can afford to fund only one goal, choose your retirement over college costs. This may sound selfish, but it makes sense. Here's why: Your dollars work harder in a retirement account such as an IRA or 401(k) because the earnings aren't taxed until you withdraw them. Plus, with most 401(k)s, your employer makes matching contributions. This results in a higher total return than you could possibly achieve in an individual investment plan lacking these advantages. In addition, colleges rarely count retirement savings when determining your eligibility for financial aid.

Here's the clincher, though. In the end you alone are responsible for ensuring that your retirement will be comfortable. Commercial lenders won't bankroll you, and you certainly don't want to panhandle your kids. Meanwhile your child can tap into myriad sources of money for college, including scholarships, work-study programs, and loans at preferred rates, with a lifetime to pay them back. If you end up enjoying a plush retirement, you can take over your child's loan payments, if you choose.

By mastering these ground rules, you will avoid the most common financial mistakes made by parents of college-bound children. Now you're ready to consider the following specific investment guidelines for children of various ages. To see how the advice plays out for specific families, see the profiles and portfolios on pp. 52–58.

Newborn to Age Eight: Go for Growth

For a running start, stash up to 100 percent of your savings in domestic and international growth stocks. The greater your tolerance for risk, the higher your commitment can be.

You've got the time to live through any market volatility, so now's your chance to plunge into growth stocks. Investment advisers urge parents of young children to put as much as 75 percent of their college money in at least two U.S. growth stock funds, 10 percent to 25 percent in one or more international stock funds, and the rest in a short- or intermediate-term bond fund. While growth-oriented stock funds are subject to price swings that historically average nearly 16 percent, you have time to ride out the inevitable drops and capture stocks' historically high long-term returns.

If you've never invested in a fund, Susan Belden, senior editor of the monthly newsletter *No-Load Fund Analyst* ($195 a year; 800-776-9555), recommends that you start with a fund that has some international exposure and a manager with a strong track record. Her choice: Mutual Qualified (no-load; $1,000 minimum investment; 800-553-3014). The conservative growth-and-income fund has raked in 15 percent annual gains over the past decade, yet it's 33 percent less risky than other funds of its type, according to Chicago fund rater Morningstar.

When you have more money and more experience, you'll want to assemble a diversified fund portfolio. To make this task easier, Table 5-1 on page 60 indicates what size companies different funds invest in. Look under the table's Style column, next to each fund's name, to make your selections: large-cap funds that concentrate on corporations with market capitalizations over $5 billion; midsize funds (market capitalizations of $1 billion to $5 billion); and small-cap funds (under $1 billion). Generally, small-company stocks are more volatile than midsize ones, and midsize shares are more mercurial than the large-caps, which include such stalwart household names as General Electric and General Motors.

Also in the Style column, note what investment philosophy characterizes each manager's approach. There are two basic choices: growth, whose followers look for stocks with strong earnings potential; and value, whose adherents seek out shares they think are trading at prices that understate a company's true worth. (Some managers follow a blend of both approaches.)

Why pay attention to stylistic details? The reason is results: growth and value approaches don't move in lockstep. In 1991, for instance, the average growth-oriented fund gained 37 percent, compared with 29 percent for its value peer, according to Trinity Research, a financial management and research firm in Boston. Then, in 1992, value delivered a 12.4 percent return vs. only 5.7 percent for growth-oriented funds. Over the past 25 years the value approach has turned in a 12 percent average annual gain, three percentage points higher than growth-oriented funds. In any one year, however, it's a horse race as to whether the growth or value funds will nose out the juiciest gains.

When it's time to make the final cut, the funds that you choose should depend on your youngster's age and your willingness to take risks. For a toddler, the professionals advise that you divide your money between growth and aggressive-growth funds. For children in grade school, you might put about two-thirds of your domestic funds in a large-cap portfolio and a third or so in a small-capper, choosing funds with contrasting styles—growth, value, or a mix of the two. With a careful blend, you don't have to rely on picking the right fund at the right time.

After you make your U.S. choices, invest up to 25 percent of your stake in an international stock fund. Foreign markets don't necessarily move in sync with Wall Street, so you'll get diversification to help smooth market bumps and grinds, along with potential for strong gains.

Over the past decade Morgan Stanley's index of European, Australian, and Far Eastern stocks—commonly called the EAFE index—gained an average of 18 percent annually, compared with 14.6 percent for Standard & Poor's index of 500 large U.S. firms. Ibbotson's Scott Lummer expects international stocks to post strong annual returns averaging 13.5 percent over the next five years.

If you can withstand the occasional market squall for the chance of a flight to the moon, advisers suggest that you put some dollars in a fund that specializes in the emerging markets of countries in Africa, Latin America, or Asia. These volatile economies, which have been growing at twice the rate of the developed countries, can take fund investors on one memorable market ride.

Consider, for example, Montgomery Emerging Markets (no-load; 800-572-3863)—a fund too volatile to make our table on page 60. It dances to an exotic rhythm: after a stunning 59 percent gain in 1993, Montgomery dipped to an 8 percent loss in 1994 as Mexico's woes threw most emerging markets into reverse, then dropped 9 percent in 1995 for a three-year annualized return of 10 percent. Respectable, but hardly sizzling.

Nonetheless, such funds are expected to produce enviable returns over the next few years, as emerging nations' economies grow an average of 6 percent annually, compared with the forecasted 3 percent for developed countries. So if you like to bet a few bucks on the lottery, instead try your luck with a developing countries fund. The odds of a big score are better, and you could reap chili-hot returns.

If you're an investor with no stomach for risk, however, the Ibbotson advisers recommend stashing the final 10 percent of your portfolio in bond funds. While bond returns are expected to be more modest than the gains of your equity investments, a small dose of fixed income smoothes volatility, making for a more stable portfolio than one that's all in stocks.

If you're a novice investor on a small budget, and the thought of choosing a fistful of funds makes you queasy, consider the one-shot remedy. Begin by placing your bet on a fund that mimics a widely used index of stocks, which could become your portfolio's keystone. One favorite of investment professionals: Vanguard Index 500 (no-load; 800-851-4999), which mimics the Standard & Poor's 500 and registered a 16.5 percent annualized return during the past 5 years through 1995. Its solid results come in part from its anorectic .19 percent expense ratio, which is less than half the average expense ratio for mutual funds tied to the S&P. Moreover, the Vanguard fund clocked in with 14 percent less volatility than the average equity fund.

Even if you balk at tying your fortunes to the bouncy S&P, you cannot retreat to the safety of bank CDs. Begin instead with a highly conservative fund, like one of the equity total-return funds in our table. Many of them managed to break even or notch slight gains in the rough 1990 market. But after a year of experience in the market, step up to more aggressive choices. A conservative total-return fund will probably advance at a decent trot but won't gather sufficient speed to get you to your goal on time.

Ages Nine to 13: A Delicate Balance

To keep your stash growing safely in these middle years, start moving toward a half-and-half mix of stocks and bonds.

With five to 10 years before your first college bill, continue to steer at least half of your new investment dollars into stocks. The shorter your time horizon, though, the more you need to start backing away from equities.

At this stage you must start trading off the possibility of high returns for greater predictability of outcome. Take a more cautious approach, locking in gains and making sure you don't suffer big losses as college draws nearer. If a severe bear market hits you at this stage, you won't have enough time to reverse the damage with aggressive-growth stocks. By the time your child becomes a teen, start moving about 15 percent of your stock holdings a year into more conservative investments.

During this period, consider gradually beefing up your holdings of fixed-income securities. The goal: to have your assets about evenly split between stocks and bonds by the time your child enters high school. One easy way to achieve this redistribution is to direct roughly three-quarters of your new savings into balanced mutual funds, which typically keep 25 percent to 40 percent of their portfolios in bonds. The interest income from the bonds helps to cushion losses when equity prices fall.

Alternatively you can continue to hold separate stock and bond funds but move money from small-company or international funds to less volatile large-company funds. "That way you'll be more conservative, but not so cautious that you lose growth altogether," says Lisa Osofsky, a financial planner for M. R. Weiser & Co. in Iselin, N.J. Another less chancy option: Buy equity-income funds. By seeking income as well as capital gains, these funds give you a cash cushion as insulation against market bumps.

Ages 14 to 18: Into the Last Laps

Preserve your profits by gradually shifting from stocks to fixed-income and cash investments.

As you get closer to the first college bills, gradually head for the off ramp, exiting stock funds for safer havens. By the time your son or daughter turns 16, the pros advise that you have 40 percent to 45 percent of your portfolio in low-risk equity total-return funds. For a jolt of higher-octane growth, sock 5 percent to 10 percent in a growth-and-income fund. In recent years the typical growth-and-income fund gained 9.3 percent, compared with about 8 percent for equity total-return funds and 11.5 percent for aggressive-growth funds.

Stash the remainder of your savings in U.S. Treasury funds. The bulk of your fixed-income investment belongs in securities with average maturities of 10 years or less. Ibbotson recommends that a small portion be allocated to higher-yielding long-term issues. But by heavily weighting your bond holdings to intermediate- and short-term issues, you will avoid steep losses if interest rates rise sharply. For example, the price of a 30-year bond will fall 10.8 percent if rates rise one percentage point, while a 10-year issue will dip a less disastrous 6.8 percent, and a five-year issue will slump only 4 percent.

Most of the time you don't give up much yield for being cautious about maturity. Not long ago the 6.75 percent yield on a five-year Treasury security equaled 91 percent of the yield on a 30-year issue.

If you are in the 28 percent federal tax bracket or higher, tax-exempt municipal bonds can be more advantageous than Treasuries. A 5.4 percent yield on a five-year muni is equivalent to 7.5 percent on a taxable bond for investors in the 28 percent bracket, 7.8 percent for those in the 31 percent bracket, and 8.9 percent for high-income investors in the 39.6 percent bracket.

Some parents might want to consider Series EE U.S. savings bonds for their college funds. The interest on these issues, sold for half the amount they are worth at maturity, is free from state and local taxes. If you hold the bonds for less than five years, you will earn a variable rate pegged to 85 percent of an average of six-month Treasury bill yields. Recently that would work out to around 4.75 percent. After that period you earn 85 percent of the average yield of five-year Treasury notes. Uncle Sam promises that bonds will reach face value within 17 years—which guarantees a minimum return of about 4.2 percent.

While the rate of return on savings bonds may not be spectacular, if you use the bonds' interest for college, you may qualify for a special tax break that effectively increases your yield.

Here's how it works: The interest on your savings bonds for college will be fully exempt from federal taxes if you hold the bonds to maturity and your income in the year you redeem them is below a certain threshold—recently $41,200 for singles and $61,850 for couples. (The limits are adjusted upward each year for inflation.) Above these amounts the exclusion begins to phase out, and it disappears completely once your income hits $56,200 for singles, $91,850 for couples. You must secure the bonds in your name, not your child's, if you want to take advantage of this tax break.

Two or three years before college and continuing into your child's freshman year, you can keep 10 percent or so of your portfolio in conservative stock funds, but plan on being completely out of equities by the end of your child's sophomore year in college.

One cautionary note: This simple strategy is not advisable if you think your family will qualify for financial aid from Uncle Sam. In that case you should sell all the stock and bond funds on which you have capital gains by the end of the calendar year in which your child becomes a high school junior. Under federal aid formulas, you will be expected to contribute to college costs about half of any capital gains realized during the year before you apply for assistance, but only around 6 percent of your assets. For further details, see Chapter 7.

Once you've liquidated the major part of your stock fund holdings, consider putting 50 percent or more of your money in short-term bond funds with maturities of four years or less. Such portfolios commonly yield about two percentage points more than plain-vanilla money-market funds do.

A different option is to buy short-term zero-coupon Treasuries (from a bank or broker) that mature before each tuition bill. Unlike conventional bonds, zeros pay no interest along the way. Instead you buy them at a substantial discount from their ultimate value at maturity. For example, a zero that will pay you $1,000 in the year 2000 might cost around $785 now. (Check at least three brokers for the best price.) If you buy four separate zero Treasuries maturing in each of the years that your child will be in college, you'll get your money just in time to meet tuition bills.

Immediately before your child enrolls in college, start switching some cash into a money fund, so that you can write checks against it for freshman- and sophomore-year bills. The remainder of your college money belongs in CDs or zero-coupon Treasuries that will mature in time for your child's junior and senior years—and which pay more than the money-market yield. (If you like, a mutual fund of Treasury zeros or other short-term government securities will do just as well.) If you can snag a 6 percent CD, that return will almost keep you even with the anticipated rise in college costs.

• The younger your child, the more aggressive you should be in your investing style. You have time to recover from market dips.
• Like it or not, you must start with stocks. Mutual funds simplify this process for most parents, unless they are experienced investors.
• Rein in risk as your child moves into his or her high school years. This means lightening up on stocks and moving to safer investments such as short-term bond funds or CDs.

CHAPTER FIVE

Putting Those Strategies into Practice

The investment strategies described in the previous chapter can help you accumulate the money you need, whether your child is a toddler, a teen, or somewhere in between. But moving from paper money to the real thing may require a leap of faith, especially if you are a novice investor. To guide you, four model portfolios follow, designed by Ibbotson Associates, a highly respected Chicago financial research and consulting firm, for four families. The ages and financial situations of the family members are real, but their names have been changed to protect the students' privacy.

Model Portfolios:
The A's, B's, C's, and D's of Doing It Right

PORTFOLIO #1

• AIM FOR GROWTH

With two young daughters to send to college, the Able family needs to put more of their savings into growth stocks.

As an architect, Alex Able, 33, of Phoenix, knows the importance of designing an extra margin of safety into his houses. So it seems quite in character that he and his wife Alice, 39, both graduates of Arizona State University, have been supercautious in deploying the $9,700 they have set aside to educate daughters Zelina, 5, and Yvonne, 3.

Starting when Yvonne was a month old, the couple, who rely chiefly on Alex's $40,000 salary, have regularly tucked $50 a month in low-risk money-market funds for both girls. Additionally they have socked $2,000 in an equity total-return fund for Zelina and $2,000 in a growth fund for Yvonne. Unfortunately, if the Ables continue to follow their current strategy, their account for Zelina, now $5,600, will grow to just $31,000 by the time she enters college in 13 years. If college costs rise at 6.5 percent annually, as predicted, that will be barely enough to cover two years at a public school. And Yvonne's $4,100 savings is projected to increase to only $30,000 when she is ready for college.

The Ibbotson analysts recommend a far more aggressive investing strategy to help the Ables meet their goals. First the couple should boost college savings about $200 a month and commit nearly 90 percent of their money to domestic and international growth stock funds. The analysts expect the combination to gain an average of 15 percent a year. There may be some potholes in the road along the way, of course, but by diversifying among different types of stocks and bonds, Ibbotson calculates that the portfolio has only a 1 percent chance of gaining less than 2.8 percent in any one year before the girls get to college. (For funds that suit this strategy and the others in the profiles that follow, see "75 Top Funds for College" on page 59.)

GOING FOR ALL-OUT GROWTH

With college more than 10 years away, the Ables can afford to shrug off temporary market drops and invest aggressively with international and domestic growth stock funds.

Portfolio Allocation

Large-cap stocks	40%
International stocks	25%
Small-cap stocks	22%
Long-term bonds	8%
Intermediate-term bonds	5%
Projected average annual return	15.3%

PORTFOLIO #2

• CONCENTRATE ON REDUCING RISK

With a young teen starting high school, it's prime time for Bonita Baker to seek stability by adding bonds to her daughter's college portfolio.

Wendy Baker, 13, of Park Forest, Ill., fancies that she might like to be a teacher. "I'll encourage her to become a college professor," says her ambitious mother, Bonita Baker, 51, who earns around $50,000 a year selling advertising for a Chicago radio station.

Determined that Wendy should fulfill every ounce of her potential, Baker recently enrolled her in a Roman Catholic girls' high school. "I decided to spend the $3,500 a year on private school tuition rather than invest it for college," explains Baker, a single mother who earned her bachelor's degree on partial scholarship from the University of Illinois at Urbana/Champaign. If Wendy proves herself an exceptional student now, Baker reasons, she may enhance her chances of winning financial aid later.

Baker puts aside about $2,000 a year for college costs that she may personally have to cover. So far she has her stash of nearly $20,000 split evenly between a balanced fund, which invests 60 percent of its assets in large-cap stocks and 40 percent in high-quality short-term bonds, and a growth fund that concentrates on large-cap stocks.

With college bills just five years away, Ibbotson's analysts advise Baker to diversify among more asset classes to reduce risk. "There's a reasonable chance she could lose money in the next five years," says Scott Lummer, a managing director of the Ibbotson Consulting Group. Lummer wants her to boost her bond investments from 25 percent to about 45 percent of her total portfolio and then move half of her equity money into small-cap and international funds.

Ibbotson analysts project that this combination of investments would cut Baker's average annual return from 13 percent to 11.8 percent. But the mix would also decrease her portfolio's volatility by 27 percent. The analysts figure that Baker would run just a 1 percent chance of earning less than .5 percent in a single year, and they estimate that her account could reach $35,000 before Wendy heads off to college in five years.

This amount probably won't cover all the costs at a public school, and the Bakers would definitely require financial aid if Wendy chooses a private college. But Baker professes not to worry: "I know we'll work it all out," she says.

BE CONTENT WITH CONSERVATIVE GROWTH

With college bills looming in just five years, the chief goal is to avoid big losses by keeping your portfolio diversified.

Portfolio Allocation

Large-cap stocks	27%
International stocks	18%
Small-cap stocks	9%
Intermediate-term bonds	25%
Short-term bonds	13%
Long-term bonds	8%
Projected average annual return	11.8%

PORTFOLIO #3

• DIVERSIFY THE INVESTMENT MIX AS COLLEGE NEARS

Three undeveloped residential lots, worth about $45,000, constitute the Cruz family's chief investment. With son, Victor, starting college in three years and daughter, Wanda, in six, the Cruzes need to sell the land quickly, and put the proceeds into more liquid investments.

Carlos and Cecilia Cruz of Miami never earned college degrees, but they are determined that their son, Victor, 15, and daughter, Wanda, 12, will. To pay the bills, the parents are banking on their children qualifying for financial aid. "This is like a gamble," says Carlos, 40, a $43,000 distribution clerk for the U.S. Postal Service.

Indeed it is—and a bigger one than the Cruzes may realize. Based on today's criteria, the family would probably have to cover at least two-thirds of Victor's costs at a Florida state college, estimates Karen Fooks, financial aid director at the University of Florida in Gainesville.

The couple's chief investment is three undeveloped residential lots totaling seven acres situated in Daytona, Naples, and Palm Beach. The Cruzes paid $22,500 for the land about 20 years ago. Today, Carlos, a part-time real estate broker, estimates the value has doubled to about $45,000. "Every time we bought land, we were thinking of the kids' future," says Carlos. "We knew land would be difficult to sell, so we wouldn't be tempted to raid the investment for other things."

Exactly because land is so illiquid, Ibbotson analysts advise Carlos and Cecilia, 38, a part-time sales clerk, to put it on the market at once. When the parcels are sold, the Cruzes should put the proceeds in a liquid portfolio that they can begin drawing upon when the kids start college. Since Victor will be ready in just three years, the Cruzes ought to invest the money for two goals—his looming college bills and Wanda's in six years. To meet those needs, Ibbotson recommends that half the money be put in conservative bond funds and the rest in growth-oriented stock funds. By adjusting the balance annually so that the fixed-income portion increases by about 5 percent a year, they will progressively safeguard their assets as college nears. And on the chance that scholarships, financial aid, and the family's savings won't cover all his college costs, Victor, a second-tier black belt in tae kwon do, is prepared to kick in and help cover some of the college costs by teaching the Korean martial art.

SEEKING GAIN WITH SAFETY

With two kids headed for college at different times, the Cruzes need a 50-50 blend of stocks and bonds in their portfolio.

Portfolio Allocation

Large-cap stocks	26%
International stocks	16%
Small-cap stocks	8%
Intermediate-term bonds	27%
Short-term bonds or cash	15%
Long-term bonds	8%
Projected average annual return	11%

PORTFOLIO #4

• GET SERIOUS ABOUT SAVING—AND GET INTO STOCKS

With one daughter in junior high school and two youngsters following behind, the Drapers need to step up contributions earmarked for future tuition bills.

David and Deborah Draper are giving their children—Sarah, 12, Roger, 10, and Patti, 2—the type of idyllic upbringing that seems characteristic of the *Father Knows Best* era rather than the rambunctious 1990s of *The Simpsons.* Their three-bedroom home in Beaver County, Pa., is on a peaceful road next to a dairy farm. Sarah and Roger attend top-quality public schools, while Deborah, 38, spends her time caring for baby Patti. They live comfortably on the $58,800 salary that David, 41, earns as a project manager at an engineering firm.

They have one major worry, however. "My biggest financial concern is not being able to afford the kids' college education," says David. The first bills to arrive will be for Sarah, Deborah's daughter from her first marriage, which ended in divorce. Sarah will be ready for college in six years, and young Roger will follow three years later.

The couple expects to realize $20,000 in the near future from the sale of a two-bedroom house that was Deborah's during her first marriage. The couple have invested their all-purpose retirement and emergency savings fund of $109,000 mostly in money-market and fixed income holdings. Realizing that he must up the ante to cover the three kids' projected 12 years of college costs, David estimates he can start contributing a maximum of $400 a month to a college fund for the three kids. The family has a good chance of qualifying for financial aid, at least during the year when both Sarah and Roger will be in college.

Ibbotson's analysts suggest that the Drapers assume more risk for the sake of growth. The blend they recommend: 65 percent in stocks, 35 percent in bonds and cash. To increase their potential for strong returns, Ibbotson further advises that fully 41 percent of the money be invested abroad, in a mix of international equities and bonds.

SEEKING MORE GROWTH WITH SAFETY

With three kids to educate, the Drapers must steel themselves to put more money into equities in order to meet the cost of their education. If all the kids go to a public school like nearby Penn State, where one year of tuition, fees, and room and board now runs $15,370, the family would be looking at a total bill of $184,440—at today's prices. Fortunately, three-quarters of the students at Penn State get financial aid.

Portfolio Allocation

Large-cap stocks	33%
International stocks	21%
Small-cap stocks	11%
International bonds	20%
Short-term bonds/cash	15%
Projected average annual return	12.9%

75 TOP FUNDS FOR COLLEGE

With more stock and bond mutual funds (6,458) than four-year colleges (2,149), building a college investment portfolio is arguably as challenging for parents as choosing the right school is for their kids.

To make your selection easier, here is a quick guide to 75 of the best. Their credentials: Each has beaten its category averages for the past three years. The portfolio managers have at least three years of experience. Finally, the funds are less volatile than their peers. Thus these funds will help you take as little risk as possible with your college savings, while still giving you an excellent shot at above average gains. (Column three lists each fund's risk level, as calculated by Morningstar, the Chicago fund rating service; 1 is the lowest risk, 12 is the highest.)

To help you balance your portfolio, we divided the funds into six asset categories—domestic stocks, international stocks, short-term bonds, intermediate-term bonds, international bonds, and real estate funds. "Real estate is a major world-asset class, so to be well diversified, investors should include it in their portfolios," says Roger Gibson, head of Gibson Capital Management of Pittsburgh and author of *Asset Allocation: Balancing Financial Risk* (Irwin Professional Publishing; $45). Gibson suggests investing in domestic stocks first, since that should be the largest asset class in your portfolio, then adding domestic bonds for balance, international stocks, real estate securities, and international bonds.

Our stock funds include top performers that charge sales commissions (or loads), as well as ones that don't. We confined our bond picks to no-loads, however, because fixed-income funds with the same maturity and quality characteristics produce much the same returns. All funds are ranked in order of the highest to lowest three-year performance.

Table 5-1

Fund	Type	Style	Risk level	% annual gain (or loss) to July 1, 1995			% yield[1]	% max. initial sales charge	Annual expenses (% of assets)	Minimum initial investments	Automatic investment minimums (initial/monthly)	Telephone (800)
				One year	Three years	Five years						
DOMESTIC STOCK FUNDS												
Neuberger & Berman Focus	Gro	Lg/Val	9	26.4	19.3	15.5	0.7	None	0.85	$1,000	$50/$50	877-9700
Omni Investment	Gro	Sm/Val	N.A.	15.1	18.0	11.4	0.0	None	1.43	3,000	3,000/100	223-9790
Mutual Qualified	G&I	Md/Val	4	19.9	17.9	14.9	1.4	None	0.73	1,000	1,000/50	553-3014
Mutual Beacon	G&I	Md/Val	3	16.3	17.8	14.1	1.2	None	0.75	5,000	5,000/100	553-3014
Mutual Shares	G&I	Md/Val	5	20.6	17.1	14.2	1.4	None	0.72	5,000	5,000/100	553-3014
Gradison-McDonald Est. Value	Gro	Md/Val	6	21.3	17.1	12.2	1.8	None	1.20	1,000	1,000/50	869-5999
Reich & Tang Equity	Gro	Md/Bl	4	25.1	16.4	13.6	3.8	None	1.17	5,000	N.A.	676-6779
Neuberger & Berman Partners	Gro	Md/Bl	9	24.0	16.0	13.2	0.5	None	0.81	1,000	50/50	877-9700
Clipper	Gro	Lg/Val	10	29.1	15.5	14.7	1.2	None	1.11	5,000	5,000/150	776-5033
Oppenheimer Growth A	Gro	Lg/Gro	10	29.5	14.9	13.9	0.7	5.75	1.07	1,000	25/25	525-7048
Quest for Value A	Gro	Md/Val	9	24.9	14.6	13.5	0.6	5.50	1.71	1,000	50/50	232-3863
Oppenheimer Total Return A	G&I	Md/Bl	9	15.8	14.6	12.8	2.4	5.75	1.01	1,000	25/25	525-7048
Affiliated	G&I	Lg/Val	6	23.3	14.0	12.2	2.5	5.75	0.63	250	250/50	874-3733
Dreyfus Core Value Investor	Gro	Lg/Val	9	20.5	13.9	9.3	1.3	None	1.11	2,500	100/100	782-6620
AARP Growth & Income	G&I	Md/Bl	6	19.0	13.7	13.3	2.9	None	0.76	500	50/50	322-2282
United Income	ETR	Lg/Bl	8	21.3	13.7	12.0	1.2	5.75	0.74	500	50/25	366-5465
Scudder Growth & Income	G&I	Lg/Bl	7	18.7	13.5	13.5	2.6	None	0.86	1,000	1,000/100	225-2470
Washington Mutual Investors	G&I	Lg/Val	7	22.0	12.8	12.0	3.2	5.75	0.69	250	50/50	421-4120
Pilgrim America MagnaCap	G&I	Lg/Bl	9	20.6	12.5	10.9	1.0	5.00	1.53	1,000	100/100	992-0180
Massachusetts Investors A	G&I	Lg/Bl	8	20.5	12.4	10.9	1.9	5.75	0.71	1,000	50/50	637-2929
Stagecoach Corporate Stock	G&I	Lg/Bl	8	24.7	12.1	10.8	1.6	None	0.97	1,000	100/100	222-8222
IDS Stock A	G&I	Lg/Bl	7	14.9	12.1	11.5	2.5	5.00	0.76	2,000	100/100	328-8300

Fund	Type	Style	Risk level	% annual gain (or loss) to July 1, 1995			% yield[1]	% max. initial sales charge	Annual expenses (% of assets)	Minimum initial investments	Automatic investment minimums (initial/monthly)	Telephone (800)
				One year	Three years	Five years						
First Union Value A Investment	G&I	Md/Val	7	21.4	12.0	11.0	2.6	4.75	0.93	1,000	1,000/25	326-3241
Penn Square Mutual	G&I	Lg/Bl	7	18.7	11.8	11.0	2.0	4.75	0.99	500	500/100	523-8440
American Mutual	G&I	Lg/Val	6	17.8	11.7	11.1	3.5	5.75	0.60	250	50/50	421-4120
Investment Co. of America	G&I	Lg/Bl	8	19.5	11.7	11.3	2.4	5.75	0.60	250	50/50	421-4120
Dean Witter Dividend Growth	G&I	Lg/Bl	7	20.1	11.3	11.1	1.9	5.00[3]	1.42	1,000	1,000/100	869-3863
IDS Equity Value B	G&I	Lg/Val	8	10.7	10.6	11.4	1.9	5.00[3]	1.56	2,000	100/100	328-8300
STANDARD & POOR'S 500 INDEX				26.3	13.2	12.7						
RUSSELL 2000 INDEX				20.7	16.5	12.9						
INTERNATIONAL STOCK FUNDS												
Sit International Growth	Intl	Lg/Gro	10	7.6	14.9	N.A.	0.3	None	1.65	2,000	500/100	332-5580
Vanguard Intl. Growth	Intl	Lg/Bl	11	7.1	12.8	5.9	1.3	None	0.46	3,000	3,000/50	851-4999
Warburg Pincus Intl. Eq. Common	Intl	Lg/Val	12	(4.4)	12.4	9.0	0.7	None	1.44	2,500	2,500/100	257-5614
USAA International	Intl	Md/Bl	11	4.2	12.0	7.9	0.0	None	1.31	1,000	1,000/50	382-8722
Hotchkis & Wiley Intl.	Intl	Md/Val	11	11.1	11.7	N.A.	2.5	None	1.00	5,000	N.A.	346-7301
T. Rowe Price Intl. Stock	Intl	Lg/Bl	11	4.5	10.7	6.9	1.0	None	0.96	2,500	50/50	638-5660
Scudder International	Intl	Lg/Bl	11	3.0	10.4	5.3	0.0	None	1.20	1,000	100/50	225-2470
Fidelity Diversified Intl.	Intl	Lg/Val	12	5.5	10.3	N.A.	0.2	3.00	1.25	2,500	2,500/100	544-8888
IAI International	Intl	Lg/Val	11	0.0	9.9	6.9	0.1	None	1.72	1,000	1,000/100	945-3863
Loomis Sayles Intl. Equity	Intl	Md/Val	11	10.0	9.6	N.A.	1.0	None	1.46	2,500	1,000/50	633-3330
Quantitative Intl. Equity Ord.	Intl	Lg/Val	11	(2.6)	9.3	0.5	1.3	1.00	1.90	5,000	1,000/100	331-1244
20th Century Intl. Equity	Intl	Md/Bl	11	(0.2)	9.1	N.A.	0.0	None	1.84	2,500	50/50	345-2021
Babson-Stewart Ivory Intl.	Intl	Md/Gro	11	2.5	8.8	6.7	1.0	None	1.32	2,500	100/100	422-2766
MORGAN STANLEY EAFE INDEX				1.7	12.7	4.7						

REAL ESTATE

Fund	Type	Style	Risk level	% annual gain (or loss) to July 1, 1995			% yield[1]	% max. initial sales charge	Annual expenses (% of assets)	Minimum initial investments	Automatic investment minimums (initial/monthly)	Telephone (800)
				One year	Three years	Five years						
Cohen & Steers Realty Shares	Spec	Sm/Gro	11	2.9	14.8	N.A.	3.7	None	1.00	$10,000	N.A.	437-9912
Fidelity Real Estate Inv.	Spec	Sm/Gro	11	1.2	10.4	12.7	4.2	None	1.14	2,500	$2,500/$100	544-8888
Templeton Real Estate Sec. I	Spec	Sm/Val	10	1.2	8.5	8.8	5.4	5.75	1.03	100	25/25	292-9293
CGM Realty	Spec	Sm/Val	N.A.	5.5	N.A.	N.A.	1.7	None	1.58	2,500	2,500/50	345-4048

SHORT-TERM BOND FUNDS

Fund	Type	Average weighted maturity (years)	Risk level	% annual gain (or loss) to July 1, 1995			% yield[2]	%max. initial sales charge	Annual expenses (% of assets)	Minimum initial investments	Automatic investment minimums (initial/monthly)	Telephone (800)
				One year	Three years	Five years						
Strong Advantage	IGC	0.5	1	6.3	6.4	7.5	6.8	None	0.80	1,000	$50/$50	368-1030
Columbia U.S. Gov. Securities	Gov	1.8	1	6.6	5.0	7.2	5.4	None	0.81	1,000	50/50	547-1707
Smith Breeden S/D Gov. Series	MBS	0.5	1	6.9	5.0	N.A.	6.2	None	0.11	1,000	50/50	221-3138
Permanent Port. Versatile Bond	IGC	1.1	1	6.6	4.6	N.A.	5.5	None	0.86	1,000	N.A.	531-5142
Vista Short-Term Bond	IGC	1.2	1	6.5	4.5	N.A.	5.2[1]	None	0.31	2,500	2,500/100	648-4782
Crabbe Huson U.S. Gov. Income	Gov	1.9	2	6.7	4.5	6.7	5.4	None	0.75	2,000	2,000/100	541-9732
Preferred S/T Gov. Securities	Gov	1.4	1	5.8	4.3	N.A.	5.8	None	0.78	1,000	50/50	662-4769
20th Century U.S. Gov. S/T	Gov	1.6	1	7.2	4.2	6.3	5.6	None	0.81	2,500	2,500/50	345-2021
Dreyfus/Laurel S/T Bond Inv.	IGC	1.5	1	7.1	4.1	6.4	5.7[1]	None	0.95	2,500	100/100	782-6620
IAI Reserve	IGC	5.8	1	5.8	3.9	5.1	5.6	None	0.85	5,000	1,000/100	945-3863
Eaton Vance S/T Treasury	Gov	0.6	1	5.9	3.7	N.A.	5.3	None	0.60	5,000	50/50	225-6265
Neuberger & Berman Ultra Short	IGC	0.8	1	5.5	3.6	4.9	5.7	None	0.65	2,000	50/50	877-9700
LIPPER SHORT-TERM U.S. GOV. INDEX				7.7	4.7	6.9						

Fund	Type	Style	Risk level	One year	Three years	Five years	% yield[†]	% max. initial sales charge	Annual expenses (% of assets)	Minimum initial investments	Automatic investment minimums (initial/monthly)	Telephone (800)
					% annual gain (or loss) to July 1, 1995							
INTERMEDIATE-TERM BOND FUNDS												
Scudder Zero Coupon 2000	Gov	5.0	7	11.9	9.2	10.7	5.4	None	1.00	1,000	1,000/50	225-2470
Benham Target Maturities 2000	Gov	5.5	7	13.5	9.1	11.0	5.8	None	0.59	1,000	1,000/25	331-8331
Strong Gov. Securities	Gov	8.8	2	13.5	9.1	10.4	6.6	None	0.90	1,000	50/50	368-1030
Steinroe Income	IGC	7.3	3	12.8	8.7	10.1	6.9	None	0.82	2,500	1,000/50	338-2550
Heartland U.S. Gov. Securities	Gov	8.1	7	9.3	8.3	10.1	6.5	None	1.07	1,000	50/50	432-7856
Vanguard F/I Intm.-Term	Gov	7.5	4	13.2	8.3	N.A.	6.4	None	0.28	3,000	3,000/50	851-4999
Rushmore U.S. Gov. Intm.	Gov	8.9	6	14.3	8.1	9.4	6.0	None	0.80	2,500	500/50	343-3355
Fidelity Inv. Grade Bond	IGC	9.5	3	9.5	8.1	9.9	6.3	None	0.75	2,500	2,500/100	544-8888
Harbor Bond	IGC	7.6	2	10.6	7.8	10.4	6.7	None	0.77	2,000	500/100	422-1050
Premier Managed Income A	IGC	9.8	4	10.0	7.7	9.4	N.A.	None	0.98	1,000	1,000/100	554-4611
Columbia Fixed-Income Securities	IGC	6.2	3	12.4	7.6	9.7	6.7	None	0.66	1,000	50/50	547-1707
Vista Bond	IGC	8.4	3	12.2	7.4	N.A.	N.A.	None	0.31	2,500	2,500/100	648-4782
LIPPER INTERMEDIATE-TERM U.S. GOV. INDEX				9.1	5.7	7.8						
INTERNATIONAL BOND FUNDS												
T. Rowe Price Intl. Bond	WI	7.3	7	17.3	10.9	13.4	5.8	None	0.98	2,500	50/50	638-5660
Benham European Gov. Bond	WI	6.4	9	18.5	10.6	N.A.	6.7	None	0.86	1,000	1,000/25	331-8331
T. Rowe Price Global Gov.	WI	6.9	3	12.5	7.3	N.A.	5.9	None	1.20	2,500	50/50	638-5660
Warburg Pincus Global F/I	WI	5.2	5	6.2	6.4	N.A.	9.8	None	0.95	2,500	2,500/50	257-5614
Bull & Bear Global Income	WI	6.6	10	4.5	5.7	7.3	4.2	None	1.98	1,000	100/100	847-4200
Scudder Intl. Bond	WI	8.2	7	3.9	4.2	10.8	6.6	None	1.27	1,000	1,000/50	225-2470
LIPPER INTERNATIONAL BOND FUND INDEX				1.8	9.8	5.5						

Notes: N.A.: Not applicable; Intl: International; MBS: Mortgage-backed security; Spec: Specialty; WI: World income; Styles: Bi: Buys stocks that blend growth and value characteristics; Gro: Buys companies with accelerating earnings; Lg: Buys stocks with total market values over $5 billion; Md: Buys stocks with total market value between $1 billion and $5 billion; Sm: Buys stocks with total market values under $1 billion; Val: Buys stocks that are inexpensive relative to their earnings or assets. **Source:** Morningstar Inc., Chicago, Ill.; 800-876-5005. [†]12-month distributed yield; [‡]30-day SEC yield; [§]Maximum deferred sales charge **Types:** ETR: Equity total return; Gov: U.S. Government bond; Gro: Capital growth; G&I: Growth & income; IGC: Investment grade corporate;

CHAPTER SIX

Demystifying the Financial Aid System

Paying for your child's college education on your own may feel as likely as single-handedly retiring the national debt—so be thankful that it's probably not necessary. You know there's help there: more than $46 billion from Uncle Sam, the states, and the colleges. But how to unlock the coffers successfully?

Taking a first glance at the process, you may feel confused and strangled by red tape. Worse yet, you worry that you and your child may jump through the hoops of paperwork only to emerge empty-handed. Maybe the bonus you got last year for selling the most widgets will count against you. Perhaps the financial aid officer will reject you and your offspring because all your savings went to fund your retirement account—while you neglected to save for college. Or just maybe you have a good salary, but it took every penny, including the widget bonus, just to keep the family afloat.

Familiar concerns? A pervasive fear of middle-class parents is that their incomes are too high for their kids to qualify for financial aid. While it's true that some government programs (notably Pell Grants) reserve their help for the most needy students, a lush array of other public and private options remains. Even with an income of $100,000 and modest assets, your family may still receive financial assistance, especially if you have two or more children attending college or if your student is unusually appealing to a particular school. If your income is $50,000 or less and you have few assets beyond your home, your child is virtually certain to qualify for some form of help.

You might take heart from this example: At Harvard recently, the average family income of scholarship students exceeded $60,000. In certain circumstances the university made awards to families with incomes above $100,000. Approximately 70 percent of students received financial aid—and the total average financial aid package, including grants, loans, and term-time jobs was $18,000.

If you're blessed with a brainy kid, your chances of winning a handsome aid package improve. "Most aid is still need based, but colleges are giving increasing consideration to merit," says Sandy Baum, chairman of the economics department at Skidmore College. "Often it shows in the mix of financial aid packages. The college may award a bright student with financial need more grant money, then offer a mediocre applicant assistance in the form of loans or a work-study job."

Your chief weapons in this war will be your child's brainpower (or athletic, musical, or other ability, in some cases), your family's economic circumstances, and your persistence in pursuing all opportunities. Wielding all three assets to the max, you may be able to capture far more aid than you and your family dreamed possible. It can be a laborious process, but don't lose sight of this essential truth: The opportunities that financial aid offers far outweigh the headaches it may provoke. The system is one you can master and work to your advantage.

Before starting your campaign to win that money, however, school yourself on the three broad categories of help that are available for undergraduate students.

• *Scholarships and grants,* also known as gift aid, are the most prized form of help, because the student never has to pay back the money. The cash may come from the federal government, the state, the college, the local Kiwanis Club, or even your friendly local car dealer.

Sometimes the dollars come in the form of a tuition discount given by the college, so technically no money changes hands. One generous example: Students who rank among the top 10 of their class academically at any public high school in the United States can attend New York's Bard College (recent cost: $27,499 annually) for the same amount charged by the applicant's state university.

• *Education loans* are usually subsidized by the federal or state government or by the college, though there are some private lenders as well. Their interest rates are lower than commercial loan rates; repayment typically doesn't begin until after the student graduates or leaves school.

Parents, if they so choose, can borrow the entire cost of their child's education, minus any financial aid. But have your child exhaust his or her borrowing ability first, even if you plan to make the payments on his or her behalf. Reason: Students get a lower rate on federal loans and often can defer interest payments.

Even better, a handful of employers, such as Kaiser Permanente, the giant California-based health organization, are agreeing to help new employees pay their education loans. So there's a slim chance you or your child could slip off the repayment hook—but don't count on many companies to show that kind of generosity.

• *Student employment* or work aid is another form of self-help financial aid. The Federal Work-Study Program and college-sponsored programs usually require students to put in 10 to 15 hours a week for a salary at or near the minimum wage. If the student is lucky, the job will have some relationship to his academic interests. Otherwise the college will assign the recipient to simple grunt work like filing or groundskeeping. One financial break: The IRS doesn't require students to pay Social Security tax on wages they earn in jobs provided by the colleges and universities they attend, including jobs in the Federal Work-Study Program. (Jobs with other employers are subject to Social Security tax withholding.)

Where the Money Comes From

FINANCIAL AID FROM UNCLE SAM

The U.S. Department of Education is by far the largest single source of student assistance, providing $35 billion annually, or about 75 percent of all financial aid dollars, to undergraduate students. Not all colleges and universities take part in all the federal programs, however, so your child should contact the financial aid office of the particular schools that interest him or her to find out precisely what is available.

To make matters more complicated, Congress changes the ground rules on federal financial aid periodically. Your starting point, therefore, is to send for a copy of the free booklet *The Student Aid Guide,* which Uncle Sam updates every year (U.S. Department of Education, Federal Student Aid Information Center, P.O. Box 84, Washington, D.C.; 800-433-3243). Recently, of course, congressional budget cutters have been taking aim at federal aid to education, so programs are subject to change. For now, though, here's Uncle Sam's menu of offerings:

• *Pell Grants,* named for Senator Claiborne Pell, who wrote the legislation that created them, are the first and largest source of federal grant money. In a typical year, more than four million students share over $5.7 billion of Pell money. The Department of Education guarantees Pells to every student who meets the financial qualifications.

The maximum amount of the grant varies every year,

depending on the funding that Congress appropriates, but the amount your student could receive depends principally on your family income and costs at your child's college. The average Pell Grant was $1,545 in the 1994–95 school year, though the range ran from $100 to about $2,350. Uncle Sam pays the grant funds directly to the college, which then credits the student's account. Pells are typically awarded to undergraduates who show exceptional need—often from families with annual income of $35,000 or less—so don't factor them into your planning if you're well above that range.

• *Supplemental Educational Opportunity Grants,* sometimes referred to as Supplementals, are also reserved for students with exceptional financial need. Unlike Pell Grants, however, Supplementals are not guaranteed to every eligible student. The Department of Education gives each school's financial aid office an annual lump sum to distribute as it wishes, with certain restrictions. When the dollars run out, Uncle Sam doesn't replenish the money until the next academic year—a compelling reason to ensure that your child applies early. The maximum award a needy student can receive is $4,000, but the 1995 average was a parsimonious $745. Most schools award Supplementals in the $500 to $1,000 range so they can help greater numbers of needy applicants facing unexpected emergencies.

• *Perkins Loans,* named for the late Kentucky congressman Carl Perkins, is a third federal program for undergraduates with strong financial need. The special attraction of the Perkins is its gentle interest rate—a modest nip of only 5 percent, the lowest of any education loan. Repayment usually begins nine months after the student graduates or leaves school. The Perkins, in addition, has especially generous conditions for deferring repayment, reducing the amount of the debt, or even canceling it if the graduate serves as a Vista or Peace Corps volunteer or teaches certain subjects. If a borrower simply experiences economic hardship, he or she can apply for easier repayment terms.

Eligible undergraduates may borrow up to $3,000 a year in Perkins Loans, with a maximum of $15,000 for an undergraduate degree. The government hands out the money to the schools, which then select the recipients and specify the loan amounts.

One tip: If the college your child is considering has a default rate below 7.5 percent (the financial aid office can supply this bit of information), he or she may be able to borrow somewhat larger amounts than the average $1,342 Perkins Loan. Uncle Sam rewards efficient financial aid administrators by supplying periodic infusions of new capital to lend out. And because dollars from past loans are regularly being repaid to the revolving fund, colleges with low default rates can afford to offer more generous Perkins Loans to the new generation of entering students.

• *Subsidized Stafford Loans,* named for Vermont senator Robert Stafford, take a bigger repayment bite than the Perkins Loans. Still, their variable rates are sufficiently low that they remain a good deal for needy students. The Stafford's interest rate is pegged to the three-month Treasury bill rate, plus 3.1 percentage points, with a cap of 8.25 percent. Maximum loan amounts range from $2,625 for a freshman to $5,500 for juniors, seniors, and fifth-year undergraduates.

The federal government subsidizes the Stafford Loan rate for needy borrowers by paying the interest while the student is in school and during a six-month grace period after graduation. (Unsubsidized Stafford Loans, in which the borrower owes interest from the day the check is issued, are available for students without financial need. These loans are discussed in Chapter 9.) If your student qualifies for a Stafford, note that he or she will also pay an origination fee and insurance premium of up to 4 percent of the amount borrowed, which is subtracted proportionately from each payment before your child gets the money. The Stafford subsidies have been under strong congressional attack lately, so double-check that the government-paid interest period while the student is in school survived the most recent federal budget cuts.

• *Work-Study programs* are a form of working your way through college with federal assistance. Uncle Sam awards each school an annual lump sum to pay 75 percent of salaries for needy students who work on campus or, sometimes, off campus for a public agency or a private nonprofit organization. The typical weekly workload is 10 to 15 hours, though there is no strict limitation. A few lucky students toil at jobs related to their majors. The second-best slots are ones that provide occasional quiet moments for on-the-job studying. Still, many students are assigned to routine tasks. When you and your child visit colleges, take a look at the phone answerers, library aides, or drivers of transportation shuttles. You're probably seeing work-study in action.

Students can use their earnings to cover whatever expenses they like. The average 1995 pay: $1,065. The money comes as straight salary, with no fees or commissions allowed—and no overtime work, either.

Although Uncle Sam reserves most taxpayer dollars to pour into need-based aid like the Pell and Perkins programs, some juicy prizes are available to reward academic achievement. Your child's high school guidance department should be able to provide details, or call the Federal Student Aid Information Center (800-433-3243). Here is a rundown of the federal government's major merit-based offerings for undergraduates:

• *Robert C. Byrd Honors Scholarships.* Grants of $1,500 a year to outstanding high school graduates, renewable annually for four years. Congress allocates funds to each state on the basis of its school-age population. The states establish their own criteria for handing out the money. Students who have already completed a year or more on the scholarship are funded first; the leftover money is awarded to incoming freshmen. For example, in 1995, California funded 2,293 scholars (the largest number in the nation), including 770 new students, with its $3,439,000 allotment. Vermont and Wyoming had just 42 students apiece. All the state agencies handed out a total of $29.1 million in Byrd scholarships in 1994–95.

• *National Science Scholars.* Grants to honor outstanding achievement in the physical, life, or computer sciences, mathematics, or engineering. The maximum potential grant is $5,000 (or the cost of attending the college, whichever is less), renewable for four years. The actual amount varies according to the funding Congress appropriates each year. In 1995 science scholars (generally two from each congressional district) won $3.3 million in grants, with an average award of $2,750.

• *National and Community Service.* The Americorps program, inaugurated by President Bill Clinton soon after he took office, has been under attack by Congress, and it appears to face a cloudy future. In 1994, however, about 20,000 young volunteers gave nine months to community programs in one of four priority areas: education, human services, the environment, or public safety. For their efforts, Americorps volunteers receive a living allowance of $7,500 and another $4,725 toward college costs or payment of student loans. Students must complete 1,700 hours of service work per year. They can work before or after they go to college or graduate school. For more information, call 800-942-2677, or write Corporation for National and Community Service, 1100 Vermont Ave., N.W., Washington, D.C. 20525.

Finally, of course, there is the military option, which provides a generous payoff if your son or daughter is willing to tote that gun, get that haircut—and can meet the stiff physical and academic requirements. The Reserve Officers' Training Corps scholarships help pay your child's way at participating colleges and universities. The United States service academies prepare young men and women for careers in the military, the Merchant Marine, or the Coast Guard.

• *Reserve Officers' Training Corps (ROTC).* If your John or Jane is in top physical and academic shape and willing to accept appointment as a commissioned officer in the military after graduation, Uncle Sam will pay virtually all costs for his or her education. ROTC scholarships typically cover 80 percent to 100 percent of college tuition, books, and fees—and provide a monthly stipend for four years of college. In recent years the federal government has handed out around $131 million annually to future officers, with an average annual payoff of $8,000 to each recipient. Qualifying physical and academic standards vary somewhat among the colleges, but they are uniformly tough. High SAT scores (1,250 or better), combined with an interest in math, science, or engineering, will strengthen your child's chances of winning a scholarship. Varsity sports participation is another plus. The military will provide a list of colleges and universities that offer the program, and your child seeks admission on his or her own. Specific requirements and awards will vary among the different branches of the military. High school guidance departments and local recruiting offices can provide further information.

• *The service academies.* The U. S. Military Academy at West Point, N.Y., the Naval Academy at Annapolis, Md., and the Air Force Academy outside Colorado Springs, Colo., make up the big three in this group. Students who make the cut have only to pay a onetime fee of $1,500 on arrival. After that, tuition, room, and board are free and those who stay the course get a modest yearly salary.

The chief hurdle, of course, is getting accepted. Applicants must be nominated, usually by their U.S. senator or representative, but the president and certain other dignitaries also enjoy the privilege of naming candidates. The nominees undergo the same type of admission screening conducted by highly selective colleges, must pass a physical fitness test, and must meet immutable height and weight requirements. If your child is short, obese, or married, squelch any dream he or she has of attending. On average, an elite 15 percent of students applying to the big three make it into the entering class. Graduates pay back their schools by serving time on active duty. The U.S. Naval Academy and the U.S. Air Force Academy require six years. Graduates of the U.S. Military Academy serve six active years and two in the reserves.

Admissions procedures are slightly different for the remaining two institutions—the U.S. Coast Guard Academy in New London, Conn., and the U.S. Merchant Marine Academy at Kings Point, N.Y. Appointments to the Coast Guard Academy are based on national competition for admission, a process that resembles applying to a selective college, and no political nomination is required. The Merchant Marine Academy, like the big three, requires a nomination by your senator or congressional representative. Tuition, room, and board are free, but students must pay an annual fee, recently $800. They earn no salary but do collect a stipend during shipboard training.

AID FROM THE STATES

All states maintain extensive programs of grants, scholarships, loans, and fee reductions at in-state institutions. On the whole, though, they reserve their funds almost exclusively for eligible students who are legal residents of the state and plan to attend college there. A handful of states, however, including Alaska, Massachusetts, and Ohio, have signed reciprocity agreements with one or more others that permit "exchange student" programs. A few, such as Minnesota, permit students living near the state's border to study in the adjoining state at in-state tuition prices.

Since the most substantial subsidies at state universities are for native sons and daughters, brace yourself if your teen is dreaming of Michigan and you live in Kansas. The distinguished Ann Arbor university presents out-of-state students with a tuition bill of nearly $16,000, rivaling the rates of many private institutions. And Michigan taxpayers don't cotton to the idea of subsidizing visiting Kansans, no matter how bright they are.

At last count, more than 20 states provide home-grown academic talent with some type of financial incentive to attend in-state schools. Some state help is relatively restricted. There might be special assistance to the children of veterans or deceased police officers, for instance, or help for students who agree to work in-state after graduation in priority areas such as teaching or health care.

A few states, including California, New York, Michigan, and Pennsylvania, are known for innovative, generous programs that help a broad range of youngsters. Georgia provides an inspiring example with its HOPE (Helping Outstanding Pupils Educationally) program, financed by the state lottery. In 1995–96 the Peach State expected to distribute $120 million to 125,000 students.

Your child's high school guidance office should be able to supply up-to-date information for all the sources and varieties of state aid for your aspiring collegian. Make sure you inquire about aid from the State Student Incentive Grant program, which is funded jointly by the U.S. Department of Education and individual states—each of which has its own name for the program, as well as its own eligibility criteria, award amounts, and application procedures.

If you have trouble getting the facts you need, call the Federal Student Aid Information Center (800-433-3243) to obtain the name and number of the appropriate agency within your state's department of education. Then request information about the state's financial aid programs, eligibility requirements, and application deadlines. Make sure your child completes the paperwork on time. That's advice you hear constantly, of course, but it's especially relevant to state aid, where the dollar amounts are almost always limited and run out quickly.

FINANCIAL AID FROM COLLEGES

Assistance programs sponsored and administered by colleges and universities account for around 20 percent of the total aid pie. College-sponsored financial aid usually comes from one of two sources—tuition revenues or contributions from private donors. Many institutions still tie most of their scholarships and grants to financial need, of course, but these days a bigger chunk of the colleges' own money is going into some form of merit scholarships. Loans and student jobs continue to account for the bulk of aid, but fully 25 percent of the money handed out by colleges in 1995 came in the form of scholarships. The average award: $4,600.

Cynics call it "buying students," but as competition for the best applicants increases, the institutions are using their own money to fill their classrooms with bright freshmen with diverse talents. From the colleges' view, this benefits all concerned. The best professors want to teach the cream of students. These gifted undergraduates often go on to become alumni of distinction, making notable contributions to society and reflecting further glory on their alma mater.

You may be wondering if your child is a strong enough student to secure a merit scholarship. The definition of that will vary according to the academic standards of the college and of the high school from which he or she graduates. As a rule, though, John or Jane will qualify with a B average in high school and a score of 1,000 or better on the Scholastic Assessment Test. Your youngster can improve his chances of winning merit money, however, if he sets his sights on a college where his academic excellence makes him a standout. In concrete terms, his SAT scores should probably be in the top 20 percent of the applicant pool.

As a practical matter, this tactic is worth considering only if the college is one that your child can be happy attending and is appropriate to his goals.

Remember, however, that pure academics isn't everything in the world of college aid. Colleges love to brag about the diversity of their student body, so a bassoonist from Elk Point, N.D., or a champion skier from Hungry Horse, Mont., could turn out to be the answer to an admissions officer's prayer. After all, every institution wants the brightest, most talented and distinctive freshmen it can lure—and preferably from all 50 states.

Pay particular attention to the scholarships available at each school, which guidebooks will describe. These provide an important window to what a college values most and may suggest a good match for your soon-to-be freshman. For instance, Case Western Reserve University in Cleveland annually awards $8,000 each to certain students who demonstrate distinguished achievement in dance, theater, and art. Hartwick College in Oneonta, N.Y., offers up to $6,000 a year to exceptional musicians and $7,000 to entrants who have accomplished an exceptional leadership task in high school, such as reforming their student government.

If your Jane or John has been garnering academic honors since grade school, an excellent way of snagging a serious-money scholarship is to win admission to one of the 436 honors programs at state colleges. For that, he or she will need a grade-point average of at least 3.5 and combined Scholastic Assessment Test scores of 1,150 or more. The perks: Your child will enjoy the privilege of special seminars with leading professors, individual tutorials, and the company of peers with equal brainpower. Moreover, honors students are often permitted to register for classes before other students are—a crucial matter at large public universities where courses required for graduation fill up fast.

Even better, he or she will become eligible for scholarships that are often the richest the school can offer. For example, Boston University offers trustee scholarships covering tuition and fees (recently $19,700) that are renewable annually if the recipient maintains a 3.5 grade-point average. Ohio University's Honors Tutorial College awards many of its 200 students $1,000 to $1,500 a year, and some also qualify for school year or summer research apprenticeships paying $3,000. Among the outstanding programs are those at Arizona, Clemson, Colorado, Delaware, Florida, Georgia, Indiana, Maine, Michigan, Pennsylvania State, Pittsburgh, Texas, Utah, and Washington.

The key to unlocking the merit aid coffers at private colleges, says Skidmore College's Sandy Baum, "is to investigate absolutely all the help that's available." High-cost private schools like Skidmore have developed many programs that are not need based. "Ask about the criteria, the forms, talk to the people in the financial aid office as soon as you decide to apply," Baum advises. "A letter is fine, but if you're really interested, a phone call is better. And junior year is not too early to start." Make sure your precollegian finds out what the criteria and deadlines are for such programs and obtains the required forms.

Finally don't overlook family plans. Nearly 70 colleges and universities discount tuition for the second member of a family who attends at the same time. In addition, about 75 colleges offer discounts if young John or Jane enrolls at your alma mater. Indiana's Franklin College, for one, sets aside $2,000 a year for each alumni child or grandchild, renewable annually with a B average. Small, private liberal arts institutions are the likeliest places to ferret out special family plan discounts.

PRIVATE AID SOURCES

Thousands of private groups—including corporations, charitable foundations, and civic and professional groups—offer scholarships and grants, and their aid can sometimes spell the difference between your child attending his or her dream school or shuttling to a commuter college near home. This is especially true if your child doesn't demonstrate overwhelming financial need, as defined by the government and the colleges, but definitely needs help to cover those pesky extra fees and expenses, not to mention the occasional pizza bash.

If your child is willing and able to aim high, there are a few big-buck awards that will really (or nearly) lift the financial burden from your shoulders. Here are four corporate and private scholarships that represent the cream of the offerings. High school guidance departments can supply further details about how to apply for these awards.

• *National Merit Scholarships.* Each year 15,000 students nationwide who ace the Preliminary Scholastic Assessment Tests (PSATs) are selected as semi-finalists for a National Merit Scholarship. Every state has an allocation of semifinalists based on the size of its high school population. Consequently, winning scores will vary according to how tough the competition is in a given state, but recent winners scored 197 to 221 out of a possible 240 points. Semifinalists are invited to submit applications for awards ranging from $1,000 to $8,000 each. (Financial support comes from about 200 colleges and 400 private companies.) Final selections are based not only on test scores, but also on recommendations, community service activities, and academic performance. Ultimately, about 6,700 students are tapped for a prize. To get Johnny or Jane in the running, make sure he or she takes the optional PSATs in junior year of high school.

• *The Coca-Cola Scholars Foundation* awards grants of $20,000 apiece to 50 high school seniors who have demonstrated civic responsibility, leadership, and academic achievement. One hundred runners–up receive $4,000 each.

• *The Tylenol Scholarship Fund,* sponsored by McNeil Consumer Products (part of Johnson & Johnson), pays $10,000 to each of 10 high school seniors who demonstrate leadership skills and community involvement, along with solid academic achievement. Five hundred runners–up receive $1,000 each.

• *The Westinghouse Science Talent Search* culls around 1,500 students from the eager seniors who participate in high school science fairs. This pool is invited to submit research projects in science, math, or technology. The top 10 winners receive $10,000 to $40,000 each, while 30 runners–up win $1,000 apiece.

For the average John and Jane, however, the real money is likely to be found closer to home, often collected in dribs and drabs, or offered for some qualification on which the college places a premium. George Washington University in Washington, D.C., for example, awards $3,000 to each of 17 cheerleaders. Virginia's Lynchburg College gives out $2,000 to $8,000 to nine students who are skilled musicians. Here are four other little-known scholarships that might enrich your Johnny or Janie's educational future:

• *Harness Tracks of America* (602-529-2525) awards five annual grants of $3,000 each to sons and daughters of licensed drivers, trainers, breeders, and caretakers or to young people engaged in harness racing.

• *The Voice of Democracy program,* sponsored by the Veterans of Foreign Wars (816-968-1117), offers 52 scholarships of up to $20,000 to students who best express their patriotism in a three-to-five-minute audiotaped essay.

• *The Adams Family Association* (946 Morgan Ave., Chattahoochee, Fla. 32324) may award your child some money if you show financial need and are a descendant of Jesse Allen Adams (1791-1866) and Elizabeth Bryant (1792-1832).

• *The Western Golf Association Evans Scholars Foundation* (708-724-4600) has been sending caddies to college since 1930. The Evans Scholarship is a one-year grant that covers tuition and housing; it may be renewed for up to four years. The chief requirement: Applicants must have caddied successfully and regularly for at least two years. The winners, about 250 annually, must attend specific colleges within their state. Ohio residents, for example, have a choice of Ohio State, Miami University, or Oxford University.

There are, all told, more than 300,000 opportunities out there to garner free money. The trick, of course, is finding the ones for which your scion might qualify. Daunted by the complexity of the search process, many parents simply pay someone else to do the looking for them. You can go that route, of course, and there are plenty of commercial services that will take your dollars to do computer searches for scholarships. The value of the information they provide varies widely, however. Keep in mind as well that only about 1 percent of the $46 billion in financial aid awarded in 1994–95 came from third-party sources.

If you should decide to consult a commercial search firm, the College Scholarship Service has drawn up a list of questions it suggests you ask when evaluating a group's services:

- If the company asserts that large amounts of financial aid currently are not being used, how does it document the statement?
- Is there a minimum number of sources provided by the company? Does the company maintain its own file of sources, or does it draw on the file of some other service?
- How successful have previous participants been in obtaining funds from aid sources identified by the company?
- Will the company refund the program fee if aid sources are incorrectly matched with the student's qualifications, if aid sources no longer exist or fail to reply to the student, or if application deadlines for aid sources have passed when the information is received?

Even if you do obtain a list of organizations that offer qualifying grants, your child will still have to apply and convince those groups that he or she deserves their dollars.

You might do better to save your cash and have John or Jane undertake a computer search using one of the software packages available in many high school guidance offices or in public or academic libraries. (The College Board and Peterson's both produce respected programs that offer comprehensive national lists.) The applicant enters a complete personal profile, and the machine comes back with a list of what's out there that he or she might qualify for. Finally, John or Jane must request information from the organizations, study their criteria, and write applications for the grants.

If no computer programs are available to your child, seek out books on the subject, a few of them written by former students who scored big at this game. The all-time winner is probably Marianne Ragins of Macon, Ga., one of five children of a widowed seamstress. Driven by a genuine need for money, coupled with first-class brains and Olympian persistence, Ragins managed to land $400,000 in scholarships. She couldn't take advantage of them all, of course, but wound up using $125,000 of the best at Florida A&M. Her book, *Winning Scholarships for College: An Insider's Guide* (Henry Holt; $10.95), lists 100 scholarship sources, along with detailed strategies on how to apply.

Be aware, however, that the bulk of private scholarships pay only enough to give a mild boost to your financial efforts. Most outside scholarships—that is, awards given by nonprofit groups, corporations, and foundations that you can use at any school of your choice—are generally no more than $500 to $1,000. Worse, they're often for one year only. You would need half a dozen or more to make a real dent in college costs.

Moreover, your child's college may require its share of the take. At Amherst College, for instance, the policy is that the first $1,000 in outside scholarships, plus 50 percent of any additional money, goes to replace loans in the financial aid package; many institutions follow similar guidelines. (As a consequence, some freshmen neglect to report these awards to the college—a risky choice.) If your child wins a portable merit scholarship, brag to the neighbors about it, but don't expect it to work a financial miracle.

The best risk/reward bet, if you've raised a burgeoning Nancy Drew or Dick Tracy, is to encourage your young sleuth to pursue his or her own quirky scholarships, starting in the neighborhood and with groups to which your family has some affiliation. After exhausting what the high school guidance office has to offer, have him or her canvas colleges, past and present employers (yours and your child's), unions, religious groups like the Knights of Columbus, and community organizations such as Rotary or Kiwanis.

Joe Paul Case, dean of financial aid at Amherst College, advises students: "Think about factors that relate to you and your family background: your race, ethnicity, religion, intended major, career plan. You might uncover some group that offers a scholarship that your high school guidance office never heard of." Case also has a practical strategy for parents: "Have your sophomore or junior keep an eye on the local newspaper for accounts of awards to graduating seniors." A year or so later, when he or she is ready to apply to college, your child can then try to snag them personally.

• Don't rule out the possibility of financial aid just because you think your income is too high. With a diligent search of public and private sources—especially if you have a brainy or talented kid—you may qualify for a surprising amount of money.

• When studying college guidebooks, pay particular attention to the merit scholarships available at each school. These provide clues to what a college values most and may suggest a good fit for your child.

• For a premier education at public school prices, consider the honors programs at state universities. Your child has a crack at special scholarships, plus the privilege of studying with elite professors and peers with brainpower equal to his or her own.

CHAPTER SEVEN

How to Win
the Financial Aid
Game

For many parents, the major obstacle to applying for financial aid is fill-
ing out the aggravating forms. True, you need to spend a couple of hours
rounding up niggling numbers, then copying them neatly in little boxes.
Ah, but consider the possible payoff: hundreds or even thousands of dol-
lars for each hour you put in. Besides, you'll need those figures later on
to fill out your income tax return. So take the plunge, preferably in late
December of your child's senior year. Delaying may mean that the finan-
cial aid office has given away the best grants and work-study jobs, and
your child will have to make do with loans.

In principle, of course, aid officials construct all packages
strictly according to the applicant's perceived financial need. In
practice, however, there are increasing gray areas in the colleges'
own aid formulas where the aid administrator can use discretion.
If you and your student learn how to work the rules—both
written and unwritten—to your advantage, you may boost your
chances of finding one or more colleges willing to offer all the
aid you need, preferably in a package that's light on loans and
heavy on grants.

In an ideal world, of course, you could find out whether your family qualifies for aid, and for how much, before your child even makes a formal application to a college. That way you could shop around knowing how much each school would really cost. Such easy assistance exists only in your dreams, unfortunately. Financial aid officers don't give parents even a ballpark estimate up front—in part because they don't want to have to backpedal later on, when they start parceling out the limited resources at their disposal.

This doesn't mean that you are forced to shop totally in the dark, however. Colleges must use a federal formula, known as the "federal methodology" (FM) in calculating what a family must shell out and how much help Uncle Sam will give. For an approximation of what the government will require as your "expected family contribution," as it's formally called, take a look at Table 7-1. To obtain a more precise estimate, sharpen your pencil and fill out the worksheet that follows. A processing office will calculate the exact number after you formally apply for aid, a procedure that we will explain in detail further on.

ESTIMATE YOUR SHARE OF THE COLLEGE BILLS

This table will give you a rough estimate of how much colleges will expect your family to contribute to your child's college costs. The calculations are based on the so-called federal methodology—Uncle Sam's rules for determining parents' and students' eligibility for financial aid. While the formula may not reflect what you believe is your ability to pay, colleges use it to decide how much federal assistance to give your son or daughter. (Schools make their own rules about handing out their own money.)

Start by estimating your total assets. Don't include your family home or any retirement accounts on the list. You may subtract from the total any business debt, margin loans on your investments, and mortgages held on any real estate you own *except your primary residence.* Your home mortgage, auto loans, credit-card and other consumer debts are not deductible from your total assets.

Let's assume you own $75,000 in savings and investments, have a $10,000 mortgage on a summer cottage, and owe $15,000 in debt related to your printing business. Find the appropriate number—in this case $50,000 ($75,000 minus $25,000)—along the top row labeled "Assets." Then follow that column down until you reach your household income figure listed in the "Income" column at left. If your income is $50,000, then your expected contribution would be $7,914. If you have two children in college, divide that amount in half: you would owe just under $4,000 for each of them. The example assumes that the older parent in the family is age 44. If you are younger, your expected contribution would be a little larger to reflect that you have more working years left; if you are older than 44, your contribution would be a little less.

Table 7-1

Income   Assets

	$50,000	$100,000	$150,000	$200,000	$250,000
$25,000	$1,871	$2,474	$4,258	$6,837	$9,657
$50,000	$7,914	$10,734	$13,554	$16,374	$19,194
$75,000	$16,148	$18,968	$21,788	$24,608	$27,428
$100,000	$24,438	$27,258	$30,078	$32,898	$35,718
$125,000	$32,487	$35,307	$38,127	$40,947	$43,767

Source: College Money, Marlton, N.J.

FOR SERIOUS SHOPPERS:
A MORE PRECISE COST ESTIMATE

The worksheet below requires time and effort to complete, but it will give you a more accurate estimate of your expected family contribution to college costs than Table 7-1. The figures given were effective for the 1995–96 school year; expect the government to revise them slightly each year to adjust for inflation.

Complete sections 1 and 2 to establish your eligible income and assets. Use those figures in section 3 to calculate the parents' contribution. Next proceed to section 4 to tote up the student's share. By adding the parents' and the student's shares, you'll arrive at an estimate of what Uncle Sam will expect your family to pay toward your child's education costs. If that figure is less than a college's total annual cost (including tuition, fees, room, board, and an allowance for books and transportation), your child can most likely count on a financial aid package to help him or her meet the shortfall.

1. PARENTS' INCOME

Enter your adjusted gross income from your most recent tax return. _____
Subtract any child support you paid in that year. _____
Add the sum of all nontaxable income. _____
Add back deductions for IRA and Keogh contributions. _____
Subtract federal, state, and Social Security (FICA) taxes. _____
If both parents work, subtract employment expenses:
   $2,500 or 35% of the lower salary, whichever is less. _____
   Subtract your income protection allowance (from Table I). If the result is negative enter 0 on line A; if it is positive, enter the amount on line A. _____

A. $ _____

2. PARENTS' ASSETS

If your adjusted gross income is $50,000 or less and you did not itemize deductions on your tax return, enter 0 on line B. Otherwise enter the total value of your investments, including stocks, bonds, and real estate other than your principal home. _____

Add the sum of all cash, bank, and money-market accounts. _____

Subtract $38,900. _____

If the result is negative, enter 0 on line B. If it is positive, multiply by 0.12 and enter the result on line B. _____

B. $ _____

3. PARENTS' CONTRIBUTION

Enter the total of lines A and B. _____

Use this number to find the parents' expected contribution from Table II. Divide that figure by the number of family members attending college and enter the result on line C. _____

C. $ _____

4. STUDENT'S CONTRIBUTION

Enter the student's AGI as reported on his or her most recent tax return. _____

Subtract federal, state, and Social Security (FICA) taxes. _____

Subtract the $1,750 income protection allowance. _____

If the result is negative, enter 0. If it is positive, multiply by 0.5. _____

Add 35% of the student's investments and savings and enter the total on line D. _____

D. $ _____

5. TOTAL FAMILY CONTRIBUTION

Add lines C and D and enter the sum on line E. _____

E. $ _____

TABLE I: INCOME PROTECTION ALLOWANCE

Family size (Including Student)	Number of family members in college				
	1	**2**	**3**	**4**	**5**
2	$11,150	$9,240			
3	13,890	11,990	$10,080		
4	17,150	15,240	13,350	$11,440	
5	20,240	18,330	16,430	14,520	$12,620
6	23,670	21,760	19,860	17,960	16,060

TABLE II: PARENTS' CONTRIBUTION

If line A plus line B equals:	Then the parents' contribution is:
$3,408 or less	Minus $750
$3,409 to $10,000	22% of line A plus B
$10,001 to $12,500	$2,200 plus 25% of amount over $10,000
$12,501 to $15,100	$2,825 plus 29% of amount over $12,500
$15,101 to $17,600	$3,579 plus 34% of amount over $15,100
$17,601 to $20,100	$4,429 plus 40% of amount over $17,600
$20,101 or more	$5,429 plus 47% of amount over $20,100

Source: College Money, Marlton, N.J.

Once you've made a preliminary estimate of your expected family contribution, you can come up with the second key number in the aid game: your financial need. This will vary depending on the cost of the institution. Example: Your expected family contribution is $8,000 and the annual tab to attend Ivy U. is $28,000; your need is $20,000. At good old Sunflower State, however, where the bill is a modest $12,000, your need would be only $4,000. While the amount of your expected contribution should be roughly the same at all colleges, your need will rise or fall according to the colleges' sticker prices.

In addition, there's an extra financial twist to consider. Let's assume Ivy's old grads are a distinguished group who over time have given large sums, enriching Ivy's endowment. Using its own funds, Ivy may offer a gilt-edged trustees' scholarship of $20,000 to meet your child's need, while state-supported Sunflower, with limited financial resources, can offer a package of only $2,000 in grants and $2,000 in loans. Then, of course, the expensive school becomes the cheaper choice to attend.

There's one more preliminary step to factor into your college calculations. When your child has narrowed the choices to a handful, investigate the colleges' policies in handing out their own funds. One method is to study the financial aid information for clues. There might be special scholarships for premeds, or thespians, or talented musicians. The institution might be eager for students who will add economic, geographic, or racial diversity. A conversation with a financial aid officer and a close reading of the admissions literature should give you a feeling for what the college prizes most.

Use this information to emphasize your child's strengths on the admission forms. Make sure your Jane or John stresses any academic, leadership, musical, athletic, or other special gifts that she or he brings to the party. Jane may not realize that her account of the day she soloed for her pilot's license at age 16 would be interesting to college officials. When it comes to references, urge John to solicit among people who know him well— not your colleague Mr. Banker, or Congressman Big Deal, but individuals who can write with firsthand knowledge and enthusiasm about why he is special.

In filling out the colleges' aid forms, you and your student can provide in a supplementary letter more detailed financial information than is required by the worksheets. Note any special family circumstances, such as unusually high expenses associated with a permanently disabled younger child or support for an aging parent.

Finally, encourage your child to apply to two schools where he or she seems likely to rank in the top 25 percent of the first-year class. This will increase the odds of getting at least one significant aid offer. If your child prefers the college that makes the stingier bid, you may be able to use the other school's richer package as a bargaining chip.

To ensure you cover all the bases, obtain the complete financial aid package from every college. You'll only have to fill out the federal financial aid form once, but if any of your child's college choices require their own financial statement (and many do), you'll have it on hand.

Keep plugging away on the paperwork, even if you're convinced that your family will never qualify for aid. There are two reasons to push on. First, even if you're right, that you have too much income or assets to qualify for need-based grants, your child might land some merit aid. Second, the chances are good that you're going to need to do some borrowing before this odyssey is over. If you don't fill out the Free Application for Federal Student Aid, commonly called the FAFSA in the aid trade, you can't qualify for any of Uncle Sam's student and parent loan programs.

Filling out Those Fussy Forms

THE GAME STARTS WITH THE FAFSA

This federal application form is available at high school guidance offices (or call the U.S. Department of Education at 800-433-3243). It's the jumping-off point for all federal assistance and a lot more besides. Mainly the FAFSA is used to calculate the parents' and student's share of educational expenses. The sum of the two adds up to that key number, the expected family contribution (or EFC, as it's called).

Remember, the EFC is not a prediction of how much cash you can siphon out of a year's paychecks. Rather it's Uncle Sam's measure of your family's ability to absorb some portion of your child's educational expenses. You can cover your share through saving, if you start early, or through borrowing. If you're truly flush, you might be able to cover the EFC out of current income—but not many families do these days.

Pick up a copy of the FAFSA well in advance of need—your child's sophomore year is not too soon, or certainly in the first part of his or her junior year. Then you can familiarize yourself early on with the questions asked. (A new FAFSA is issued for every academic year, but generally any changes are minor.) At the appropriate time—typically January 2 of your child's senior year—file the form, even if you don't think you qualify for need-based aid. Colleges use the information in processing applications for federal loans that are available to all students and their parents, as well as for parceling out some state aid and merit awards.

The official deadline for filling out the FAFSA is May 1. Don't postpone this task, however, thinking you'll complete this bit of drudgery when the daffodils bloom. Federal aid forms must be processed—independent companies do the calculations, then send results to the schools—and May Day is the last day the firms handling the applications will accept them. Many colleges, however, impose earlier deadlines. March 1 is common, since many schools issue acceptances and rejections on April 15. Don't be lulled into thinking you have more time than you do. That false move could cost both you and your youngster a bundle in financial aid.

• *Calculating the parents' share.* Be prepared to bare your financial soul on the FAFSA. It asks about your income in the previous calendar year, including wages, salaries, tips, interest, dividends, alimony received, and unemployment benefits, plus capital gains on stocks, a house, or any other appreciated asset you sold.

93

In addition, you will also have to list your current savings, investments, and other financial reserves. If you study the rules in your child's sophomore year in high school (or before December 31 of his or her junior year), however, you may be able to make some sensible financial moves to protect your family assets.

The principal quirk to consider in the federal formula is this: Uncle Sam expects parents to contribute up to 50 percent of their discretionary income in any given year, but never more than 5.65 percent of their assets. Therefore you want to keep income low in the year that the financial aid officials are making their calculations. (If your graduating senior is applying for aid for the 1997–98 academic year, officers will look at your income for calendar year 1996.)

Here's one example of how this can work. If you're planning to sell an appreciated asset—shares of stock, say, or the family's lakefront cottage—do it before December 31 of your child's junior year. That way you will avoid having your onetime capital gain counted as current income just at the time when you're looking for financial assistance.

By Uncle Sam's definition, assets may include savings, stocks and bonds, equity in investment real estate, vacation properties, a business, or an investment farm. Generally exempt under the federal rules are equity in your home, pension and retirement funds, the cash value of your life insurance, vehicles, art, jewelry, and personal effects. So don't fear that Janie will miss out on all financial aid because you inherited her grandmother's five-carat engagement diamond.

When determining your expected family contribution, the college financial aid administrator will make allowances for federal and state taxes paid, unusually high medical expenses, and tuition paid for other students in the family. The officer will also make an allowance, which varies according to family size, to cover basic living expenses. (You will almost certainly find it ridiculously small.)

After subtracting these set-asides from the family's income, the aid officer considers the remaining dollars to be "available" or "discretionary" funds. Available, that is, to pay your child's education costs. The greater your discretionary income, the more of the financial burden the college will expect you to carry. As a rule, financial aid officers consider about 50 percent of your available discretionary dollars to be tappable for college bills.

To make these rather arbitrary rules less punishing, you may want to spend some money now. If you've been planning a necessary but expensive outlay, take the plunge and remove that money from the aid calculations. For example, shell out $1,000 to repair the car that John or Jane will be driving back and forth to school. If the money is sitting in his or her account, John or Jane might get $350 less in financial aid—and your entering freshman would still lack reliable transportation.

Some parents complain that the FAFSA rules penalize them for thrift. There's a grain of truth in that in the short run, but not when you take the long-term view. "Families with assets have far more choices about how to finance their share of costs," advises financial planner Raymond Loewe, president of College Money in Marlton, N.J. "And total costs end up being cheaper for them, since they don't spend years paying down heavy loan debt."

If anyone gets hit unduly hard, in fact, it may be the working student, as you'll see next.

• *Figuring the student's share.* Because students benefit directly from the educational opportunities offered, the FAFSA formula assumes that the younger generation should contribute a greater portion of income and assets than their parents are required to do. The set-aside allowances against a student's funds are much more limited, and it's likely that your John or Jane will have to contribute up to 50 percent of discretionary income, as calculated under the federal formula. In addition, he or she will have to part with a major chunk of assets: fully 35 percent each academic year. Every dollar that a working student earns above $1,750 reduces his or her aid eligibility by 50 cents. If Johnny earns a dollar and saves it, he reduces his eligibility by 85 cents. That dollar is assessed twice, 50 cents because it's income, and an additional 35 cents because it went into savings and therefore counts as an asset.

If your high schooler has some money saved, or has been stockpiling gifts from grandparents, you might let her buy her new stereo, computer, or other necessary gear before going to college, with her own money, since the aid formula will ultimately gobble more of her dollars than yours.

• *Filling out the form.* Completing the FAFSA can be tricky; read each line carefully so you don't wind up shortchanging yourself. Remember, for example, that 401(k) savings plans from employers, Individual Retirement Accounts, or other retirement savings vehicles don't count as current wealth. So don't mistakenly list them in the assets section of the form and reduce the amount of aid that you're legitimately entitled to receive.

Don't fret if you don't have the exact numbers needed on earned income, interest, dividends, and the like. Just check the box at the top of the aid request form so that officials know you are estimating. If you make a significant mistake with an estimate, you can correct it on a form you will get in the mail later on, when your W-2s and other tax documents have arrived.

Apart from that, be picky, picky, and precise in all your replies. Answer fully every question that pertains to you or your child, no matter how trivial it seems. If an answer is zero, fill in that goose egg. An empty space can trigger a computer's request for more information that can snarl your application in red tape for weeks.

Keep all possible options open. In Section C, for instance, have your child check all the boxes asking what type of financial aid he will accept. Even if he vows he would rather go shoeless than take a work-study job, have him agree to the job on paper. Financial aid directors take a more benevolent view of students who seem flexible. If the resulting aid package includes a work-study job, and your son still finds that unacceptable, he can decline that part of the package or try to renegotiate.

Finally, don't make deals with the devil when filling out these forms. You may be tempted to underestimate your income or hide some assets in hopes of getting a break on your family's expected contribution. That ploy could backfire badly, with devastating consequences for your child's future. Maybe you'll make out like a bandit the first year, but the college may well get its own back by limiting (or withdrawing) aid in future years if the deception is revealed. Financial aid directors who administer federal money are required to verify a percentage of aid applications. In these cynical days, *The New York Times* reported recently, private investigators are even called in at times to cross-check numbers.

With the FAFSA as your starting point, apply for every federal financial aid program that you learn about and report all rejections in your aid applications to colleges. A university financial aid officer may be reluctant to allocate resources to your child if he or she believes that you haven't explored every possibility. Similarly, the states will take a jaundiced view of an aid request if you haven't applied for federal money first.

NOW TACKLE THE FINANCIAL AID PROFILE

Though it was instituted only in 1995, some 800 colleges and universities, many of them high-priced private schools, now require applicants to file a new document, the College Scholarship Service/Financial Aid Profile. The new form is administered by the College Board, which charges a $5 processing fee, plus $14.50 for each copy it sends out to colleges. The reason for its swift popularity? "The federal form only shows current income," says Cathy Thomas, director of financial aid at the University of Southern California. "The new profile shows trends in finances that are informative—and sometimes results in students being eligible for more aid than under the federal formula." Then, too, they often show the opposite, since most take into account your home equity, retirement accounts, and other assets that the FAFSA ignores. In addition to the basic core of questions, the profile will probably contain sections custom tailored to the criteria of the schools to which your child is applying. The value of the profile, Thomas adds, is that it provides a far more comprehensive view of a family's financial status, rather than focusing narrowly on one year's income, as the FAFSA does.

Your child's high school guidance office can advise if any of his or her targeted colleges require the new profile. If the private colleges on your child's wish list don't use that form, chances are they employ a similar questionnaire of their own, which they will include along with the other financial aid materials.

Divorced parents may face one more hurdle in the paper chase: Some schools insist that noncustodial parents complete the Divorced/Separated Parent's Statement, available from the College Board. Private institutions often assume that a noncustodial parent will be helping to pay for college. If this is not the case, or if the noncustodial parent's help is undependable, the custodial parent should make sure the school's financial aid office knows the situation. Send this additional information to the schools directly; don't attach it to the FAFSA or the profile.

If you are divorced and remarried, be aware that your new mate becomes part of the equation, too. The federal government requires the colleges to include a stepparent's income when calculating the expected family contribution—even if he or she has no legal obligation to support the child and no plans to help fund the stepchild's higher education. The logic is this: A working stepparent contributes to the household's overall standard of living, and single parents don't have this resource.

The result of the colleges' ways of assessing your family wealth may vary in important aspects from the federal formula. The key difference is likely to be in the treatment of the family homestead. The FAFSA won't count the equity in your home as an asset, but the profile and other forms used by colleges usually do. This can result in wildly differing estimates of your family wealth—and may suggest some strategic moves on your part.

If, for example, you're relying on a home-equity line of credit to bridge any gaps left by the financial aid offers, nail down that loan before you fill out the profile or other college forms. By reducing your equity stake in your home, the loan may improve your eligibility for some forms of college assistance. Conversely, of course, you might use some of your savings or other assets to pay down your home mortgage if your top priority is to qualify for low-interest federal loans.

The College Scholarship Service provides the following detailed rundown of the most important differences you're likely to meet between the federal rules and the colleges' methodology in analyzing your family's finances.

• *Parents' assets.* Under the so-called **federal methodology (FM),** home equity is always excluded, and in some instances a family's entire net worth may be ignored. Colleges that use an **institutional methodology (IM),** however, nearly always factor in home equity, retirement accounts, and other assets omitted in the federal formula.

• *Number of family members enrolled in college.* If more than one family member is enrolled in college, each student's aid eligibility can rise markedly. Although the FM considers a parent's college enrollment, colleges that use the IM will usually not count a parent as an enrolled student and will make adjustments if other family members are enrolled less than full-time or at low-cost schools such as local community colleges.

• *Minimum student contribution.* Under the FM, if a student reports no assets and has no income from the preceding year, the student is not expected to make a contribution. Colleges that use the IM usually require a minimum contribution from the student, typically $900 from a freshman and $1,100 from an upperclass student.

• *Business losses and depreciation.* Colleges that use the IM will often scrutinize federal tax returns and disallow certain tax write-offs, such as business losses and depreciation, as offsets to income. This is particularly true if the parent is self-employed. "If a family has a negative adjusted gross income on their Form 1040, but they're showing $150,000 in deductions on their Schedule A, they must have had that money to spend," reasons USC financial aid director Cathy Thomas, citing an extreme but true example. She and her peers nationwide are intensely concerned that the limited pool of dollars available go to truly needy families, not those who are adept at making themselves appear impoverished on paper. "That sends bristles up our back," she warns.

• *Divorced and separated parents.* Under FM rules, when a student's parents are divorced or separated, a noncustodial parent is not required to provide information (or contribute money). If a custodial parent has remarried, the family must include the stepparent's income and asset information. Colleges that use the IM may request detailed information from noncustodial parents and factor in a contribution from them if the analysis shows they are capable of paying.

WHEN TO FILE THE FORMS

The week between Christmas and New Year's is a perfect time to tackle the paperwork, Scrooge-like though it sounds. Reason: You may not mail the FAFSA until after January 1, but January 2 is an ideal time to do so, ensuring that your submission lands at the top of the heap. Save all records, such as W-2 forms, bank statements, and other materials used in completing the application. If verification is required, and you don't provide it, you won't receive aid from Uncle Sam and possibly not from other sources.

Even colleges that impose a February or March deadline for aid applications still encourage high schoolers to apply as soon as possible after January 1. If you wait for April 15, when you have completed your tax return (and when many college acceptance letters go out), you and your student could be left waiting and fretting for some long, uncomfortable weeks.

Expect your FAFSA application to be processed in about four weeks. Then you'll receive a Student Aid Report in the mail, listing your **expected family contribution** (the magic number used to determine your eligibility for federal aid). Each school listed on the application will receive the same information. If you apply electronically, your application will be processed in about a week. If you filed the profile, you will receive a separate acknowledgment for that form from the College Scholarship Service.

After the Student Aid Report is officially distributed, the financial aid process at the colleges where your child has applied can get rolling. If you and your offspring filed in a timely manner, you will have the satisfaction of knowing that the colleges considered your applications on their merits, and that the school did not reject you because it ran out of cash. Tardy applicants risk finding that the lushest grants and the most rewarding campus jobs are long gone and they must settle for loans.

When the award letters arrive, you and your student will probably find that the financial aid offers fall somewhere between 65 percent and 100 percent of your child's estimated need, depending on the colleges' own policies and the dollars in its coffers. If your need is not fully met, it means you've been "gapped," as they say in the aid biz. Gapping has become increasingly common: in the 1994 survey by the National Association of College Admission Counselors (discussed in Chapter 2), 65 percent of college and university respondents, including both public and private four-year institutions, acknowledge that they practice gapping to some extent. Of those that report its use, 64 percent apply it to all students, 23 percent to those less academically qualified. So if there's a gap between your family need and the cost of attendance, there's a chance that your child is not a high-priority candidate at that school and you'll have to look for more money elsewhere.

If more than one award is coming your child's way, scrutinize the offers with a cold eye. Don't get bedazzled by big numbers. Pay particular attention to how much of the offer is made up of grants and how much of loans that must be repaid. Is the college tossing in special awards for academic or athletic merit? If scholarships are offered, are they renewable? Check out the loan interest rates and compare the payback requirements.

If you and your child find the award from his chosen school is agreeable to you both, have him or her sign the acceptance documents included with the award notice. If the offer letter from a high-priority school was a major disappointment, consider appealing to the financial aid officer. Will it succeed? Let's explore that question in the next chapter.

• Study the FAFSA early—preferably in your child's sophomore year. You have time then to make some legitimate financial moves to protect your family wealth.

• Persist in filling out those forms—even if you think you won't qualify for aid. Chances are good that you may need a government loan before all the bills are paid. You can't qualify for any federal parent or student loan programs without first filling out the FAFSA.

• Students are expected to kick in a hefty share of their own assets and income, if any. If your child has been stockpiling cash gifts in a college fund, consider letting him buy a computer, car, or other necessary gear with his own money before going to college. The aid formula will ultimately gobble up more of his savings than yours.

CHAPTER EIGHT

Appealing Your Financial Aid Award: The Key Strategies

There's a saying among those in the aid trade: When awarding money for programs they administer but don't fund (such as federal loans), colleges give priority to the neediest of the able. When awarding dollars from their own funds, colleges give priority to the ablest of the needy. That's a useful guideline if you're considering an appeal to improve your child's financial aid award.

Simple economic reasons are forcing many private colleges to be more flexible on aid bargaining. The federal government has been shrinking its grants programs as Congress works to balance the budget. To make up the slack, colleges are kicking in more of their own money. In 1987 colleges anted up 16 percent of total aid money, while Uncle Sam ladled out 78 percent. By 1994, just seven years later, colleges were putting up 20 percent of the total, about a $3 billion increase.

Because colleges and universities must stretch their own dollars further, their initial aid offers are frequently stingy. The positive side of this situation, however, is that there's built-in room for negotiation if you make a well-reasoned argument. Many colleges hold in reserve money that decisive parents can shake loose—if they negotiate skillfully.

Beyond economics, there's also the weight of the Justice Department on the parents' side now. In 1992 the department pressured a group of highly competitive East Coast colleges to stop sharing financial aid information among themselves. The practice, common for years, enabled the universities to make similar offers to promising applicants, but the Justice Department deemed this a form of price-fixing. Under pressure, the institutions ceased making parallel offers to desirable candidates.

Today a high school senior pursued by more than one school may receive offers that differ by up to $10,000 or more, and some pulling and tugging has become an accepted part of the game. A recent survey by the National Association of College and University Business Offices showed that many small, private institutions are willing to bargain down their asking prices by as much as 30 percent.

There are no guarantees that you can get such a deal, of course, but neither are there penalties for asking. Remember this: *A college will not withdraw its acceptance or cut your child's aid package simply because you challenge it.*

Further on, we'll suggest how you can devise a bargaining strategy tailored to your own situation. First, though, consider this real-life example of how one youngster saved her parents $8,000 through her own negotiating efforts:

In the spring of 1995, Harvard and Brown Universities offered 18-year-old Shannon May, of Phoenix, aid packages equal to $22,000 of their approximately $30,000 total yearly costs. This would have required her parents to ante up $8,000 a year. To counter, May faxed both schools copies of more generous aid packages offered by nine other colleges. She reminded Brown and Harvard of the 4.59 grade-point average she had earned in high school by taking advanced placement and honors courses, which boosted her record above the normal 4.0 maximum. In addition, she emphasized that her family had unusually heavy financial burdens, since an older sibling was already in col-

lege and her mother remained home full-time to care for a seriously ill child. (Shannon's father, an herb importer, earns somewhat less than $60,000 a year.)

Concrete results came fast. Brown offered to halve her parents' yearly contribution to $4,000, while Harvard reduced it by
one-quarter to $6,000. Although Harvard required $2,000 more
a year from her parents than Brown did, May chose the Crimson,
lured by its fine graduate schools in government and medicine,
which mesh with her ambition to become a diplomatic medical
adviser. If her plan unfolds on schedule, she'll have her B.A. in
1999, and her parents will have saved $8,000.

Your child may not boast Shannon May's ace credentials, but
that doesn't mean you and your future freshman have to meek-
ly accept the first financial aid package a college offers. To pry
more money from the financial aid gatekeepers, however, you'll
need to make the most of your circumstances and your child's
abilities, as May did.

As a starting point, bear in mind that your chances of squeez-
ing more money from a college are best if you can show that its
financial aid office underestimated your child's merit or your
family's need. Here are suggestions about how to do that:

• To flush out more aid on the basis of need, make a strong
point of any financial problems that have arisen since you filed
your initial application. These might include a job loss, a serious
illness in the family, perhaps damage to your home from a flood,
hurricane, or tornado.

• If you can't muster new ammunition of that sort, request
that the financial aid officer take you through the process of how
she determined your child's aid package. You might find an area
where her analysis is faulty or that she overlooked an extenuating circumstance. Your chances of success will improve if you're
dealing with a school that has deep pockets. (You can make a
rough estimate of a college's potential largesse-per-student by
dividing its endowment by its enrollment.)

• Your other principal bargaining chip is to stress your son or daughter's accomplishments. If your child is likely to be in the top quarter of the entering class, be aware that he or she is a tempting candidate to that school. One of the most effective cards to play, as Shannon May did, is a better offer from a competing institution.

Generally, though, you must pit equals against equals: mighty Stanford probably won't match a bid from Sunflower State. But if you want to sweeten Sunflower's offer, Stanford's interest could be a potent lever to use.

If you decide to appeal an offer, focus your efforts on your child's first-choice college. The goal, after all, is to attain the best possible price at the school your son or daughter desires most.

College officials suggest that the wisest approach is to initiate the discussion with an exploratory phone call to the financial aid office. Letters may raise new issues that could force a lot of back-and-forthing between the college and the family. Result: delays and mounting frustrations on both sides.

You may be tempted to make a personal visit—but aid officers say it's no more effective than a phone call and much more costly, unless you're dealing with a commuter college. (How come you can spring for the trip but can't pay for tuition?)

On the phone, in any event, you'll probably be discussing the matter with the same officer who initially assembled your child's aid package. Be polite: the officer has the power to change the offer, but you'll have to give him a sound reason. He won't be looking for it, and he won't make any change casually. Financial aid offices are working with limited funds, and if they agree to sweeten your package, it's often at the expense of someone else's.

Absolutely suppress any instinct to bully. The same officer whom you're tempted to berate will almost certainly be responsible for putting together your child's future aid packages, if he or she does attend the college. Finally, if the official denies your request, there's no higher authority (except a spiritual one) to whom you can appeal. Don't antagonize him by dropping hints that you know Important People in the Department of Education.

Once you've made your pitch with all the eloquence you can summon, follow up with a thank-you letter that recapitulates your case. Attach any documentation that's relevant to your argument—a photocopy of an aid offer from a competing school, say.

One final caveat: Remember that a typical financial aid officer in a midsize college earns about $45,000. Don't try to pluck her heartstrings with a sob story about how inflation is devouring your $80,000 salary.

• Be confident that a college will not withdraw its acceptance or take back your child's aid package simply because you challenge it.

• To make a case for a better offer, you'll need ammunition. Two tactics: Demonstrate that the school overestimated your financial resources, or show that it underestimated your child's accomplishments.

• If your child's first-choice school made a mingy offer, use superior aid packages from competing colleges as bargaining chips.

• If you can't muster a case with the above tactics, then request that the financial aid officer walk you through the process of how she determined your child's aid package. You might find an area where her analysis was faulty or that she overlooked an extenuating circumstance.

CHAPTER NINE

Low-Cost Loans to Bridge the Money Gap

Perhaps you've made valiant efforts, but your savings and outside aid just won't stretch to cover all your child's college costs. That flood of financial aid you were expecting turned out to be a trickle. Whatever the reason, you're facing a serious gap between needs and means.

Take heart: you have plenty of company. The tough reality is that even wealthy parents often can't meet the ever-spiraling cost of four years at a premier college or university.

There are, fortunately, a number of routes out of your predicament—though some are more palatable than others. Your first response, for example, might be to insist that your future freshman trade down to a less costly school. Still, the day that Johnny gets his long-awaited acceptance letter from Duke is not the ideal time to confess that a commuter college is all you can afford. If you spent years encouraging him to study hard so that he could land a spot in a competitive university, young John might reasonably conclude that you had pulled an unfair bait-and-switch tactic. Chances are you won't feel great about it, either.

Your second idea might be to rob your retirement savings or take out a mountain of loans in your own name—or both. Generous impulses on your part, certainly, but not sensible ones. Do you really want to spend your sunset years eating cat food and depending on your offspring's handouts? "It never ceases to amaze me how many parents assume the entire burden because they don't want to saddle their children with debt," says financial planner Raymond Loewe, president of College Money in Marlton, N.J. "But who's better off carrying the loans, parents who are close to retirement or kids who have their whole working lifetime ahead of them?"

Remember, it's quite possible for the kids to make their way through college with jobs and loans, but no bank is ever going to lend you money to retire on. Further, if you're feeling prosperous in the future, you always have the option (but not the responsibility) of chipping in to cover your young wage earner's loan payments.

If your student joins the ranks of college borrowers, he or she will be going with the current flow. Nowadays about half of all undergraduates go into hock for their diplomas. The debtor class of 1994 graduated owing $10,500 on average, according to the Student Loan Marketing Association (Sallie Mae). The association expects that amount to hit $13,600 for the class of 1998—a spike of 30 percent. It projects that average payments will rise to $163 a month, from $126 recently.

Fortunately, both students and parents can choose among several excellent, low-cost loan options. Your best choices, if your student can't qualify for need-based aid and you can't meet the expected family contribution that Uncle Sam assesses, are likely to be two low-interest federal loan programs—the unsubsidized Stafford and the PLUS. There are also private sources of money worth considering. Here's a rundown of the best of the bunch:

Unsubsidized Stafford Loans

Start your loan shopping with the unsubsidized Stafford, which is part of the federal government's variable-rate student loan program. Your child need not show financial need, but he or she must be a degree-seeking student who is enrolling in school at least half-time. (At schools measuring progress by credit hours and academic terms, this means at least six hours per semester or term; at colleges that count clock hours, half-time enrollment is at least 12 hours a week. Be aware, however, that some schools choose to set higher minimums than these.)

Your John or Jane can take out an unsubsidized Stafford Loan for $2,625 to $10,500 annually—the maximum amount rises as the student progresses through four years of education. The variable interest rate, adjusted every July 1, equals the three-month Treasury bill rate plus three percentage points, with a cap of 8.25 percent. The 1995–96 rate reached that limit. (Beginning July 1, 1998, the rate will be tied to the 10-year Treasury bill rate, which is usually higher than the three-month rate.) The maximum origination fee has been 4 percent of the amount borrowed, but congressional budget balancers have recently been pushing to hike it to 5 percent. To ease the pinch, the borrower pays the fee over the entire life of the loan, which can be as long as 30 years.

The same low rates apply to both subsidized and unsubsidized Stafford Loans. The difference between them is when the student starts owing interest on the debt. With subsidized Staffords, which are need based and part of colleges' financial aid packages (as discussed in Chapter 6), Uncle Sam pays the interest while the student is in school and during certain grace and deferment periods. With an unsubsidized Stafford, interest starts accruing immediately, though students can defer payments until six months after graduation. (However, he or she can choose to make interest-only payments along the way, which will reduce the ultimate amount of the debt.)

Banks, credit unions, and other private lenders make about 70 percent of Stafford Loans (both the subsidized and unsubsidized varieties). State or private guarantors administer the loans, and the federal government insures them. Uncle Sam pays the banks and the guarantors for their services. If the student defaults, the taxpayers typically cover 98 percent of the loss, so lenders earn their profits nearly risk-free.

The remaining 30 percent of Stafford Loans comes from colleges and universities that participate in the Federal Direct Student Loan (FDSL) Program, in which the lender is the U.S. Department of Education. These direct loans, made under the Federal Family Education Loan (FFEL) Program, require less paperwork than those from private lenders. In addition, they are often faster. The student gets the loan right at the school, which saves a couple of steps, so even late applicants can get paid before the academic term starts.

Your child may, however, pay a higher price for the convenience of borrowing directly from the college. If your daughter borrows from a bank or other private lender that sells its loans to Sallie Mae, a consolidation agency that services about one-third of all student loans, she can end up paying 2.25 percentage points less in annual interest than she would owe under the FDSL Program.

Here's how the savings add up: If the student borrower makes the first 48 payments on time, Sallie Mae will knock two percentage points off the interest rate for the remaining term of the loan. The agency will further lower the rate an extra quarter of a percentage point if the borrower authorizes the electronic transfer of money from his or her bank savings or checking account. Finally, Sallie Mae will forgive loan origination fees above $250 after 24 on-time payments. With credits and interest rate reductions for timely payments, your student may be able to cut the total amount repaid by hundreds or even thousands of dollars. (See Table 9-1.)

Table 9-1

FOR CHEAPER REPAYMENTS, IT PAYS TO PLAY
WITH SALLIE MAE

When your student takes out a Stafford Loan from a bank, credit union, or other private lender, ask if the loan is resold to the Student Loan Marketing Association (Sallie Mae), as many of them are. If your child makes repayments promptly, he or she could end up paying up to 2.25 percentage points less in annual interest. Here's how the savings stack up:

• If your child makes the first 24 scheduled payments on time, Sallie Mae will forgive loan origination fees above $250 under its Great Returns program..

• If he or she makes the first 48 scheduled payments on time, Sallie Mae will cut the interest rate for the remaining term of the loan by two percentage points under the company's Great Rewards program.

• If your son or daughter authorizes automatic payments from a bank savings or checking account, Sallie Mae will further lower the loan rate by an extra one-quarter of a percentage point under its Direct Repay plan.

Assuming the borrower qualifies for all three programs, he or she can expect to receive the following savings over the life of a typical Stafford Loan with a 10-year term, assuming a loan rate of 8 percent:

Amount Owed	Potential Savings
$5,000	$386
$10,000	$852
$20,000	$2,102
$60,000	$7,095

Source: Student Loan Marketing Association.

College financial aid offices can usually supply names of lenders who sell their loans to Sallie Mae. If the aid office can't help, your child can call his or her state guaranty agency. The Federal Student Aid Information Center (800-433-3243) can provide the state agency's telephone number. You can also phone Sallie Mae directly for an information packet (800-891-1409). Colleges and universities participate in *either* the FFEL Program or the FDSL plan, but not both—so your student will not have a choice once he or she picks a college.

When it comes time to repay, your student borrower will find it makes no difference if he or she has a direct or indirect Stafford Loan. The repayment terms are virtually identical. Here are the four main options:

- *Pay the same amount each month,* at least $50, for up to 10 years.
- *Pay the same monthly amount over an extended period,* $50 minimum, for up to 30 years. The borrower will pay more in total interest because of the extended duration.
- *Start with small, graduated payments* that grow over the 12-to-30-year life of the loan, depending on the loan amount. Again, the minimum is $50.
- *Pay a portion of income,* usually 4 percent to 15 percent—for up to 25 years. After 25 years Uncle Sam will forgive any remaining loan balance, but the borrower will owe income tax on that amount.

Fortunately, borrowers can switch plans after they start making repayments. Young debtors should be aware, however, that this flexibility may carry a stiff price tag. The longer the borrower stretches out the loan, the more it will cost, so it pays to choose the most aggressive plan one can afford. (See Table 9-2.)

Table 9-2

EXAMPLES OF TYPICAL BEGINNING PAYMENTS FOR DIRECT LOAN REPAYMENT PLANS

Total Debt	MONTHLY AND TOTAL PAYMENTS UNDER DIFFERENT REPAYMENT PLANS									
	Standard		Graduated		Extended		Income Contingent[1]			
							Income = $25,000			
	Per Month	Total	Per Month	Total	Per Month	Total	Option 1[2]		Option 2[3]	
							Per Month	Total	Per Month	Total
$2,600	$50	$3,148	$25	$4,008	$50	$3,148	$90	$2,867	$27	$3,937
4,000	50	5,539	25	6,637	50	5,539	96	4,613	42	6,056
7,500	89	10,650	47	12,444	79	11,355	110	9,522	79	11,356
10,000	118	14,200	63	18,185	92	16,615	121	13,451	105	15,141
15,000	178	21,300	95	27,277	138	24,921	42	22,197	142	23,126

Note: Payments are calculated using the 1994–95 interest rate of 7.43%.
[1]Assumes a 5% annual income growth (Census Bureau).
[2]Under "Option 1," the borrower always pays the formula amount; i.e. payback rate times income.
[3]Under "Option 2," the borrower never pays more than the standard 12-year amortization amount.

Source: U.S. Department of Education.

The government may forgive an unsubsidized Stafford Loan, but only under the direst circumstances: if the borrower dies or suffers permanent and total disability. The student can't discharge the loan because he didn't like the school or course program, didn't finish his studies, or didn't obtain employment after completing the degree.

Make sure your child has a clear understanding that loan payments will be one more inescapable deduction eating into his or her postgraduation paychecks. Squash now any secret fantasies John or Jane may have about ducking those onerous repayments.

Federal Plus Loans

With a PLUS (Parent Loans to Undergraduate Students) you can borrow all your child's education costs, minus any other financial aid. If, for instance, your child has borrowed $3,000 under the Stafford program toward total college costs of $8,000, you could qualify for a $5,000 PLUS through a bank or other private lender, or from the Federal Direct Student Loan (FDSL) Program, if your child's school participates in the FFEL Program. PLUS funds are available to all parents with satisfactory credit histories, regardless of need, whether or not their children have Stafford Loans. To qualify you must have no loan delinquencies of more than 90 days, and your child must be attending college at least half-time.

The government adjusts the interest rate on a PLUS each year around July 1. The amount is pegged to the one-year Treasury bill rate plus 3.1 percentage points, with a 9 percent cap. (Recent rate: 8.98 percent.) Lenders are authorized to charge up to 4 percent of the loan amount as origination and insurance fees. That's a fair deal for parents, since the PLUS rate is typically one to three percentage points lower than that for a personal loan from a bank or a home-equity loan.

Under the PLUS there is no grace period, however. Interest begins to accrue the date the loan check is issued. Repayment generally starts within 60 days after that, but parents may sometimes defer repayment of principal and interest until the student leaves school. Interest will build up over that time, however. The duration of repayment extends from five to 10 years, but the borrower must repay a minimum of $600 annually. He can prepay all or part of the loan amount without penalty.

Borrowers must certify that they will use the loan proceeds exclusively for defraying the cost of attendance at the school where the student is enrolled. Applications for the PLUS (like Staffords) are available at college financial aid offices. If the college does not participate in the direct loan program, call your state guaranty agency for a list of private lenders. (You can obtain the number of the state agency from the Federal Student Aid Information Center at 800-433-3243.)

Home-Equity Line of Credit

If you opt to tap into your own financial assets, your cheapest option is almost always a home-equity credit line. Reason: You can deduct the interest on a loan of as much as $100,000 on your federal income tax return. The home-equity loan rate typically is the prime rate plus one or two percentage points—about 10 percent in recent years. This makes the after-tax cost of such loans just a notch above that of government-backed college loans. One caution: Some lenders charge stiff up-front fees to establish home-equity lines, so be sure to compare the cost of competing offerings before signing up for one of them.

Lenders generally permit you to siphon off up to 80 percent of home equity as you need the money to meet tuition bills. (An occasional high-flying banker may offer you 100 percent of equity, but don't take that risk.) Monthly repayments can be as little as 1.5 percent of the amount you owe during months when you are short of cash. Remember, though, that this is serious stuff: if you can't meet at least the minimum payment, you risk losing your home.

If you plan to tap into multiple sources of college cash, apply first for your home-equity line of credit. For one thing, you will qualify for a larger credit line when your monthly debt payments (including your mortgage) are low. Bankers generally require that these fixed obligations total less than 40 percent of your pre-tax income.

A second reason to apply early is that your child's college may consider your stake in your home when parceling out aid from its own funds. Since a credit line reduces your home equity, it may increase your child's chances of qualifying for financial aid from academic institutions. (The federal formula for financial aid doesn't consider home equity. A line of credit won't affect Uncle Sam's estimation of your family's financial need either positively or negatively.)

Private Loan Programs

If you can't snag a low-interest government loan, or it doesn't fully meet your needs, there are a handful of educational organizations that offer loans for all or most college expenses, minus any financial aid the student receives. Many of these companies offer fairly long repayment schedules at moderate rates—from 9 percent to 13 percent in recent years. Call the loan sponsors for current rates and other details. Four examples:

• *The New England Loan Marketing Association (Nellie Mae)* offers EXCEL Loans that can run as long as 20 years. A parent (or a student who is working full-time) may borrow from $2,000 up to the full cost of the child's education, minus any financial aid received. The cost is generally 2 percent to 4 percent above the prime rate, plus a onetime origination fee of 5 percent of the loan amount. For more information, call Nellie Mae at 800-634-9308.

• *The College Board* sponsors the Extra Credit Loan, which covers room, board, tuition, and fees, minus financial aid, for up to four years. Repayments can stretch up to 15 years. The Extra Time Loan, which is similar, permits borrowing for one year at a time; you may defer repayment of principal until after the student graduates. The maximum loan duration is 10 years. Interest rates are tied to the 90-day Treasury bill rate, plus 4.5 percentage points. Call 800-874-9390.

• *Knight College Resource Group* has a number of similar offerings with maximum durations of 15 years. Like the other lenders, Knight requires a good credit history. Call 800-225-6783.

• *The Complete Source for Financing Education* offers the PLATO Loan (which is not an acronym). PLATO allows you to borrow from $1,500 to $25,000 with 15 years to repay. The borrower must have a minimum income of $15,000; parents can cosign for students. There's a onetime origination fee of 5 percent of the loan amount. Call 800-467-5286.

• *The Education Resources Institute (TERI),* the largest private guarantor in the country, offers loans for parents of undergraduates for up to 25 years to cover the entire cost of a child's education. Specific terms are set by the sponsors, primarily banks, that participate in the program. For a list of lenders in your area, call 800-255-8374.

Since all the above lenders look for a good credit history, and the Federal PLUS program also requires an acceptable credit rating, you and your spouse might want to send for your credit reports at least a month before you begin loan shopping.

There are three major reporting agencies: TRW, Trans Union, and Equifax. The College Board suggests contacting TRW first (800-392-1122). If they don't have a file on you, try Trans Union (216-779-7200) and then Equifax (800-685-1111). TRW will provide one report at no cost each year. The other two will charge a fee. You and your spouse should both sign the request and include a check for the fee amount (if applicable) plus the following information for each of you:

• Full name including middle initial
• Current address with zip code
• Verification of your current address (such as a photocopy of your driver's license, a current utility bill, or a credit card billing statement)

- Previous addresses, including zip codes, for the past five years
- Social Security number
- Date of birth

When your report arrives, check it carefully for errors. Reporting agencies often confuse consumers with others who have similar or identical names or a similar Social Security number. The report will contain detailed instructions about how to correct any misinformation in your file. Make sure to do this before applying for new loans.

Other Sources

If you still haven't squeezed out enough cash to plug the financial gap, your *life insurance policy* could be a further source of funds. The loan rates are fairly cheap—usually between 6 percent and 8 percent. You aren't required to repay the money, which could turn out to be a plus or a minus factor. The risk, of course, is that you could undermine your family's future financial security in the event of your untimely death. If you have a $100,000 life insurance policy from which you have borrowed $40,000, for example, your family or other beneficiaries will get only $60,000 minus any interest owed. This could leave your dependents in a precarious spot if you are the principal breadwinner and there's a lot of other debt outstanding.

As a different stopgap, you may want to borrow against your balance in a *401(k) retirement account* or other company savings plan. Your employer's benefits department can provide detailed information on how to set up the loan. Generally the rules permit you to withdraw up to half of your vested balance or $50,000, whichever is less. You must pay back the money within five years at the interest rate set by your plan—typically the prime rate plus one percentage point. The rate is relatively low because the remaining dollars in your account secure your loan. In addition, of course, you are paying the interest to yourself, since it goes directly into your 401(k).

Sometimes this is a great deal: if you're the lucky entrepreneur who owns the company where your account is lodged, and Harvard gives you a tuition break if you pay $80,000 up front for your daughter's tuition, dip in freely. There's probably no harm.

For most of us, however, it's a risky choice. If you fail to meet the rigid repayment schedule that your employer sets up, your loan will be considered a withdrawal and you'll owe regular income taxes and a 10 percent tax penalty if you're younger than age 59½. Also, if you leave your current employer, the loan will come due immediately, so consider how secure you feel in your present job.

For those reasons, draining your retirement funds is a last-ditch solution in many cases. You invested that 401(k) money so it would be there when you retire. You intended those dollars to be working on a tax-deferred basis to secure your comfort in later years. Skimming off your retirement money now to meet college bills defeats that original pivotal goal.

Emergency Cash

Headache time: Despite your best effort, you simply don't have the needed cash and the deadline for paying your child's college bills is looming. What to do? Take two aspirins and in the morning call two loan programs made just for parents in your situation:

• *Academic Management Services (AMS)* will charge you a $50 fee to set up a budget and installment schedule with your child's college that will allow you to pay the upcoming tuition bill over a period of 10 months. One further requirement: The college must be affiliated with AMS (more than 1,500 schools are). To find out more, call 800-635-0120.

• *The College Resource Center* will lend you a maximum of $50,000 at interest rates as low as the prime rate plus 2.5 percentage points. There is an application fee of 3 percent. You must begin repayments of 2 percent of the outstanding balance per month or a $100-a-month minimum within 45 days. Call 800-477-4977 for further details.

• If you face a daunting gap between needs and means for your child's education, first investigate the two low-interest federal loan programs—the unsubsidized Stafford and the PLUS.

• Have your child borrow as much as possible before taking on loans in your name, for two reasons. First, students get better terms than parents, and you always have the option of assuming all or part of the repayments. Second, your child has a lifetime to pay off the debt, while you have only a limited number of good earning years left. No bank will ever lend money to fund your retirement.

• If you must borrow, check your credit rating first, especially if you have a name like Smith. You may be amazed at the errors that have crept in over the years. Sweep them out before potential lenders get put off by them.

CHAPTER TEN

Innovative Ways to Cut Costs

If you fear the only way to prune your child's college costs is to be needy enough to win financial aid, you're in for a pleasant surprise. There are a variety of other means of slashing thousands of dollars from your kid's college expenses—and none of them require sacrificing the quality of his or her education. Many of the options will work for just about anyone who takes the time and trouble to seek them out.

Of course, any of these strategies can backfire if, just to save money, you push your high schooler to attend a college that he or she dislikes. So first work with your son or daughter to identify appropriate colleges—and then look for ways to cut the costs. If you and your child find a college that's a good fit and happens to be a good value, give yourselves a pat on the back. You've been first-class shoppers.

That said, here is a rundown of potential ways to save thousands of dollars:

• *A degree in three years.* A three-year degree can cut education costs by 50 percent. That's because your whiz kid will not only skip a year's college bills—saving more than $25,000 at the nation's most expensive schools—he or she also will be able to enter the work world a year early. Add the $25,000 saved to the $25,000 that a typical grad earns in the first year on a job, and you come up with the handsome sum of $50,000. In effect, you've slashed the full price of a topflight education in half.

A degree in three years cuts costs by an even greater percentage at a state university charging $10,000 a year: the $25,000 gained from a year of work, plus the $10,000 saved by knocking off the fourth year amounts to an astonishing 88 percent savings off the $40,000 cost of a four-year degree. In today's world a three-year degree can bring higher education back within the budgets of many hard-pressed middle-class parents.

Some kids relish the rapid rush to a degree, but let's face reality: the experience is not for everyone. If your child is poorly prepared for college, he or she probably won't be able to sustain the intense pace. Be aware, in addition, that there will be serious trade-offs. If your freshman or sophomore is whizzing along, piling up credits at a gold-medal pace, he or she will be forced to give short shrift to outside activities such as sports, the arts, or an adventurous social life.

For those who are highly motivated, however, and thirsting to get into the workforce, fast-forwarding through the undergraduate experience can be the ticket to their dreams. Students who were born wanting to be doctors, for example, who can't wait to start med school, may thrive at Boston University, where premeds can earn a combined bachelor's and medical degree in six or seven years, cutting up to two years off the customary eight-year stint.

Boston University's program has been in existence for about 35 years, but many other colleges have recently begun hopping on the three-year-degree bandwagon. Roughly 175 colleges, including Drury in Springfield, Mo., Middlebury in Vermont, and Susquehanna in Pennsylvania, have established three-year tracks leading to bachelor's degrees. At Northern Arizona University there's even a special dorm reserved for students enrolled in the popular three-year program.

Savings on tuition, and room and board at small liberal arts colleges, which have some of the highest tuitions in the nation, can slice $12,000 to $25,000 or more from the price of a bachelor's degree. At Middlebury the new three-year program could chop up to $18,000 off a student's bill over four years. The college isn't cutting its degree requirements. Rather, it's restructuring its academic schedule to stretch through the summer for some students, combining some courses, and asking students to increase their course load each term.

In a tuition-saving variation of the regular accelerated programs, Clark University in Worcester, Mass., offers tuition-free fifth years (worth $19,140 recently) to freshmen who maintain grade-point averages of 3.25 or better as undergraduates and go on to earn master's degrees in the school's one-year program. Following Clark's lead, Pennsylvania's Lehigh University recently adopted a similar fifth-year-free plan.

• *Attend a community college for two years, then transfer.* With this strategy your child can end up with a first-class bachelor's degree at about 40 percent off the sticker price at the degree-granting college.

Consider this: Tuition and fees at the nation's 1,000 or so tax-supported community colleges average just $1,387. That's less than half the going rate at public four-year institutions and a skinny 11 percent of the $12,432 average annual tuition and fees at private four-year colleges and universities.

Since most community college students commute from home, they also save money on room and board, which adds up to another $4,000 or so a year. Thus a youngster who spends two years at a community college, followed by two more in residence at a four-year school, can pare about $11,000 off the $27,440 average cost of a degree from a public college and a thumping $30,000 off the $65,700 cost of one from a private college.

(A note here about definitions: About 200 two-year community colleges around the nation are not state supported but privately operated. These junior colleges, as they are generally known, average $6,350 a year in tuition and fees, still a savings over private institutions but more costly than the average public school.)

One obvious question about this strategy is whether your child can get a good education at a two-year school. The answer is yes—but. Your student may have to be a self-starter, since community colleges are usually open to any high school graduate who applies, space permitting. Many of these kids didn't hit the books hard in high school, so the classroom climate may not promote high academic expectations. In addition, courses are often less demanding than those at four-year schools.

On the positive side, however, all the money you pay goes to your child's education, not to support research facilities, graduate schools, or an army of ivy trimmers. Professors won't be Nobel Prize winners or leading-edge researchers—but they may well be excellent instructors. With no publish-or-perish mandate, they can devote themselves full-time to the classroom and their students.

At the best community colleges, students find plentiful doses of individual attention, including tutoring, remedial help, and counseling—which can help unmotivated youngsters get on track. The low-pressure, forgiving atmosphere may even transform a mediocre student into a dedicated one. As for academic ambitions, about one-third of the 6 million students enrolled in two-year schools expect to move on to four-year institutions.

To successfully execute the community college strategy, however, you must make sure that the four-year school will accept the credits your child accumulates in the first two years of study.

The best way to avoid nasty surprises at transfer time is to choose the four-year school at the same time you and your child pick the community college. Before your child even makes a formal application, ask someone in the guidance or transfer office to tell you how many recent graduates went on to four-year institutions and to which ones. If you have a specific four-year college targeted, check with its admissions office about your child's chances of being able to transfer and its policy on accepting credits.

Some states simplify the process for you. In California, for instance, state community college graduates who meet specified requirements are guaranteed admission to one of the state's public four-year institutions. Florida uses identical course numbering in two-year and four-year public institutions so that students know in advance which courses satisfy transfer requirements.

In addition, community colleges often make private arrangements, called **articulation agreements,** with four-year schools to smooth transfers, usually by making sure transferred credits will be accepted at full value. Nearly every two-year school has an agreement with at least one four-year college; some have relationships with many more.

• *Consider a commuter school.* Another surefire strategy that can cut thousands of dollars from the cost of your child's degree is to have him or her enroll at a local college and live at home. There are dozens of outstanding public and private institutions in major metropolitan areas that primarily serve students who live off campus. "Top Commuter Colleges" (below) is an alphabetical listing of 20 such schools where at least three-quarters of the undergraduates commute and a minimum of 40 percent of entering freshmen graduate within six years. That's a significant accomplishment, considering that many commuting students also hold full-time jobs and that the average six-year graduation rate for all schools is around 55 percent.

TOP COMMUTER COLLEGES

Private Schools

Alverno College (Wis.)
DePaul University (Ill.)
Holy Family College (Pa.)

Iona College (N.Y.)
Polytechnic University (N.Y.)
St. John's University (N.Y.)
Suffolk University (Mass.)
Webster University (Mo.)

Public Schools

Baruch College (City University of New York)
California State-Fresno
Florida International University
George Mason University (Va.)
New Jersey Institute of Technology
University of Central Florida
University of Cincinnati (Ohio)
University of Minnesota
University of North Florida
Temple University (Pa.)

Most commuter schools are state supported, which keeps a damper on tuition prices. Many are branches of flagship state universities, such as the University of Massachusetts at Boston. Others are large, urban institutions, like Georgia State University in Atlanta and the University of Houston, where 93 percent of the undergrads live off campus. Some intellectually challenging commuter schools have flourished in the suburbs, such as George Mason University in Fairfax, Va., which draws most of its students from the outlying areas of Washington, D.C.

Technical colleges that primarily serve commuters majoring in engineering and computer science have also won renown for academic excellence. Among the elite: the private Polytechnic University in Brooklyn, N.Y., and the public New Jersey Institute of Technology in Newark.

A large number of topflight private schools with large commuter populations are affiliated with the Roman Catholic

Church. One particularly worthy of attention: DePaul University in Chicago. Its $13,086 tuition is higher than that of the typical state university, but counselors call the school a bargain because it attracts strong students.

Shopping for a commuter school is a bit different from searching for an ideal residential college. Ask about class size, majors offered, and other academic matters, of course. At the same time, though, corner some commuting students and ask about their day-to-day experience with parking and student lounges, not just faculty and classes. Says educational consultant Edward T. Custard, of Chester, N.Y.: "Where you're going to relax between classes, or park your car, may seem like trivial matters, but inadequate parking and noisy student lounges can really trip you up."

As a parent, you should also do your part to help: encourage your child to spend the extra time and effort to join campus organizations and get to know professors. He or she will have a far more rewarding college experience than the commuting students who remain stuck on Mom's cooking and hang out mainly on the living room sofa.

• *Start and finish fast.* Thousands of high school students earn credits toward college degrees by taking demanding advanced placement (AP) courses. Such courses, offered at more than 10,000 public and private schools and covering 30 subjects ranging from art history to Spanish literature, culminate in three-hour exams scored on a scale of 1 to 5.

Most of the 2,700 colleges and universities that accept AP credits require examination scores of 3 or higher, but some competitive private institutions, including Williams College and the University of Chicago, may ask for a 4 or even a 5. A few of the most demanding schools, such as Amherst, won't accept AP credits at all.

A further caution: Some schools allow kids who perform well on AP tests to skip introductory courses but still insist that they take, and pay for, four years of classes. Ask college admissions officers and department heads to clarify their policy on AP credits before you commit yourself to a school.

Even better than AP courses (though less widely available) are the intensive two-year college preparatory programs offered at about 150 public and private high schools nationwide that lead to an international baccalaureate (IB). This diploma qualifies the recipient for up to a year's worth of credits at nearly 500 colleges and universities. Be prepared, though: parents of high schoolers enrolled in IB programs often see their ambitious kids leave home by dawn's early light, not to return till dusk has fallen.

• *Consider a prepaid tuition plan.* If you have a couple of years before your son or daughter graduates from high school, a prepaid tuition plan may sound tempting. Six states—Alabama, Alaska, Florida, Massachusetts, Ohio, Pennsylvania—offered them in 1995, while Texas and Virginia have announced that they will launch programs in 1996. At least a half dozen states have legislation on the books to start them, and more are exploring the idea.

By one estimate, more than 400,000 American families are already enrolled in such plans, about half of them in the thriving $1.5 billion Florida program. The relatively new Massachusetts plan (800-449-6332) is uniquely attractive in that neither the buyer nor the beneficiary needs to live in Massachusetts and the student is eligible to transfer tuition certificates to both private and public four-year schools in the state—a total of 67 of them, in fact.

While plans vary in their specifics, the basics are quite similar. Whether your child is a tot or a teen, you contract to pay for all or part of four years' tuition at a state school at close to the current rates. Then, when your student is ready for college, you will have locked in the tuition, regardless of how much costs have risen. States may sell contracts guaranteeing that they will pay the future tuition; others offer tuition units whose value can be applied toward future costs.

The underlying financial premise behind these plans is that by pooling thousands of individuals' savings in conservative investments, the state can earn enough to cover the cost of future tuition increases.

The prepaid plans don't attract many wealthy customers, who typically are comfortable investing in stocks and bonds. And they are inadvisable for low-income families, since prepaid tuition credits directly reduce tuition costs, which in effect reduces financial-aid eligibility on a dollar-for-dollar basis. That could be a real disadvantage for students who might be eligible for grants and need-based scholarships they wouldn't have to repay.

But prepaid tuition plans have an understandably strong appeal for middle-class parents. For one thing, the states make it easy for them. Often they allow buyers to make monthly payments as low as $25 at banks, through payroll deductions or with coupon books. The process is simple enough to encourage Grandma to chip in with gifts to help educate the grandkids. For Mom and Dad it's a familiar discipline, like paying off the mortgage or the car loan. Also, there's complete peace of mind. The family has a guaranteed tuition rate, insuring their child's education against the vagaries of politicians, inflation, and price hikes over the coming years.

In addition, prepaid tuition offers another defensive bulwark: The plans protect you from yourself. Even if the boiler blows up or the kids need braces, you can't raid the fund. "It's a nice, easy mechanism for parents to save money for college," says Michael A. Olivas, law professor at the University of Houston and editor of the book *Prepaid College Tuition Plans: Promise and Problems.*

But are the plans the best way to save? Perhaps yes, if your child is three or four years away from college and you're just starting to put money aside. If you have more time to build a college kitty, however, then you can almost certainly do better by investing in stock mutual funds. Historically, stocks have appreciated more than 10 percent a year—which is three to four percentage points more than the likely return on a prepaid tuition contract. (The plans guarantee only to keep you even with state college tuition increases.)

In addition, mutual funds won't penalize you if your child

chooses not to attend college, can't qualify for admission, flunks out, or simply becomes enraged at the idea that he or she had no input into the college decision. By contrast, even the most generous prepaid plans pay only modest interest when they refund your money if your child makes other arrangements. Florida, for example, will pay 5 percent interest on your investment—but only in the event that your child wins a full scholarship, is disabled, or dies. Otherwise you simply get back what you put in. And as investment returns go, that rates a big goose-egg.

If you're considering some form of prepaid plan, scrutinize the details closely before signing up. Note especially the promised investment returns and the refund policy if your child is unwilling or unable to attend.

It may be as important, however, to analyze yourself. If you believe in layaway plans and Christmas clubs, and know you need discipline to regularly feed your nest egg—and to prevent you from raiding it—a prepaid tuition plan may be the ticket. Prepaying is a whole lot better than not investing—but at the same time, be aware that it's not nearly so efficient over the long term as investing intelligently.

• Consider the three-year degree programs that a growing number of schools are instituting.

• Take a look at nearby community colleges or commuter colleges. If your child does well, he or she can transfer to a more prestigious university and earn its degree at a cut-rate price.

• Budget carefully enough so that you don't have to pull in the reins halfway, leaving your child with the worst outcome: a degree from the local community college because you could afford to pay only for the first two years at her dream school.

• Give thought to a prepaid tuition plan if your state offers one. They're most appropriate if you have three or four years before your child graduates from high school and you're just beginning to put money aside. The financial returns aren't the best—but a prepaid plan guarantees that you can't raid the college nest egg.

ENDPAPER

VOICES OF EXPERIENCE:
How to Minimize the Emotional Cost
and Maximize the Rewards

One of the most distinctive characteristics of **MONEY** magazine is its close relationship with readers. When we put a foot wrong, they are quick to set us straight. Even better, they are generous about volunteering advice for the magazine to pass on to future readers. The college experience, in particular, has brought forth a torrent of comment, in part because it affects nearly every family at some point. Here, then, is a sampling of our readers' collective wisdom—some volunteered, some sought out by our reporters—offered with the hope that it will enlighten and enrich you and your child's college experience.

On Choosing Colleges

• Start talking about college with your child by asking questions. Begin the process by asking "why college," not "what college."

College official, Middlebury, Vt.

• Know the admissions criteria for the college, and know your child's credentials. One mother commented to me, "I knew Amy wasn't in the top 50 percent of her class, but I had no idea she was in the bottom half!"

College official, Middlebury, Vt.

• Like most parents, we had studied our children and assumed we knew them pretty well. But our quiet son, who was marked for a small college, chose the Marine Corps, followed by the University of Michigan. His actress-scholar sister with loads of friends wouldn't look at major universities we suggested and chose a liberal arts college with a famous English department. Each got it right. They confounded their elders and did well.

Attorney, Washington, D.C.

• I'd like to put in a word for the "gap year." Nowhere is it written that one must go directly to college or university. Often the pressure comes from ambitious (or anxious) parents seeking trophies or reassurance. But a year spent on a farm, behind a cash register, or in the military may do more good at eighteen than a year in a dorm, even if Mom or Dad has to defer for a while the casual reference to Junior or Susie at Stanford.

Attorney, Washington, D.C.

• Many of our friends chose state schools for their children because the colleges were cheaper and they felt educational goals were well met. But most of their kids ended up going for five years because there was no space in classes they required. When we figure in the extra tuition and the lost opportunity costs of a year on the job, we thought they got a poor "bargain."

Physician, Minneapolis, Minn.

Making the College Trip

• Take along an extra pair of socks and put it in the glove compartment. It wasn't until my son was about to step out of the car for his first interview that I noticed the gap between chinos and loafers. I managed to convince him of the virtue of socks during the college interview process. I removed mine, which he wore until 30 seconds after he was safely back in the car.

Journalist, Washington, D.C.

• Take the college trip during spring of your child's junior year. It takes time to digest impressions and make good decisions. There's no one around in the summer, and the admissions office is too busy in the fall of senior year.

Attorney, Washington, D.C.

• Think carefully about letting your younger child visit an older sibling alone at college, if you permit it at all. The overriding impression may be one of partying and sexual adventure, while the academic experience is largely overlooked.

Homemaker, Atlanta, Ga.

• Taking our daughter and two friends on campus visits, we had them all fan out, asking people, "What's the biggest campus issue?" When everyone answers, "Security," it does tell you something. It's not just about "getting in," but do you want to "get in."

College administrator, Atlanta, Ga.

• Chill out. Your kids have already developed their own sources of information that will be valued far more than any guide, brochure, or parental rumination. One thing I learned is the whole thing is rigged. The kids know what they want to do, but they're not going to turn down a free trip around New England or to the opposite coast.

Journalist, Washington, D.C.

135

About those Applications

• Parents need to be reassured that they aren't derelict in their responsibility to their kid if they don't write their kid's essays—even when other parents around them are doing so. College is about kids coming to an appreciation of their own competence. The kid can do without the extra burden of doubting whether he'd even be in the college if someone else hadn't greased him in.

History professor, Philadelphia, Pa.

• Let them be creative. One admissions officer said he would rather read an essay titled "What I Learned about Myself Cleaning out My Book Bag" than yet another "Story of My Life."

Homemaker, Atlanta, Ga.

• I really wanted my son to go to Amherst, but he seemed to find it tight, precious, clubby. He hung back on his letter, on which much would be based, and I took an active hand in its writing. He was not admitted to Amherst. He wrote his own letter to Penn and was admitted—and Penn turned out to be a wonderful choice for him. I think he loved every minute of it.

English professor, Boston, Mass.

About Financing

• Our four-year-old son inherited a $50,000 trust fund from his grandmother shortly after he was born. We invested it in stocks with an 18-to-22-year stay-in-business-and-grow horizon, like Microsoft and Disney, reinvesting all dividends (that's important). We're pleased to think we can afford Harvard if he wants it and is admitted. But it was very different for my two older daughters: We had very little spare cash then, but I promised them unleveraged bachelor's degrees. No debt in their names. That was our deal. I have the debt and am gradually paying it off.

Management consultant, New York, N.Y.

• A wonderful grandmother gave 100 shares of PepsiCo and 200 shares of Southern Co. stock to each of our children about 15 years ago. Unfortunately we put it all in their names, so they never qualified for need-based aid. It did keep us from spending it, though. But if Grandmother had kept it in her name, we couldn't have gotten our hands on it, and the kids might have qualified for some type of financial aid.

Homemaker, Atlanta, Ga.

• For our oldest son's college education, we bought a series of CDs with September maturities. Unfortunately college bills are due in early August, so we had to max out on credit cards for a month.

Insurance executive, Basking Ridge, N.J.

• My ex-husband and I had agreed to split all my daughter's college costs down the middle, but the college insisted on dealing with one parent only when it came to questions or a problem. I engineered that my ex would be the contact in our case. I figured he would more likely be late with payments than I would, so why should I be upset by dunning calls. Ultimately this backfired. One time when he was really late, the school barred my daughter from classes, which spurred her to call me. I phoned the bursar's office immediately, but I ran into the parent-of-record problem. The school official said the only person she could talk to about money was . . . my ex-husband. I finally convinced her she would have better luck with me, the paying parent, and she relented. The lesson is this: If you and your ex are splitting college costs, the more reliable parent should be the college contact. It brings more hassles but can prevent the financial crises than can wreck your child's peace of mind.

Editor, New York, N.Y.

Entering the Postcollege World

• If your child aspires in her innermost heart of secret hearts to be a world-class champion wing walker, remind her you don't get there by mowing the grass in front of the airport. The big problem today is boredom. Kids ought to take serious steps to avoid boredom, avoid boring jobs, boring work, boring spouses, boring companions, to avoid being trapped, around the year 2030, by decisions made by a naive, impetuous, hedonistic teenager. That's not easy to do.

Author/blacksmith, Tesuque, N.M.

APPENDIX

How **MONEY** Magazine Ranks the Colleges

While other publications attempt to tell you which colleges are the strongest academically, **MONEY** magazine each year identifies the best college buys—the 100 schools that deliver the highest quality education for the tuition and fees they charge. This makes the **MONEY** magazine rankings an excellent place to start your college search or to supplement information you gather on your own from schools, friends, and other sources.

The top 100 listed here are the repeat winners—the names that have consistently cropped up in the annual **MONEY** magazine rankings over a three-year period. To discover which colleges really go the distance, we gave each institution a weighting in inverse order to its appearance on the list each year. Thus, a number 1 ranking was worth 100 points; a number 100 finish was worth only one point. The maximum weighting possible was 300—which was, in fact, achieved by New College of the University of South Florida, which has led the **MONEY** magazine list since 1994. Rice University also made it three in a row in the number 2 slot. In fact, 61 of the colleges listed here are three-peats, turning up in the value rankings for each of the past three years.

The value approach adopted by **MONEY** magazine explains why the ranking that follows includes such remarkably varied institutions as nationally acclaimed California Institute of Technology (number 5) and the relatively obscure Truman State University (number 4 and known as Northeast Missouri State University until a July 1996 name change). No one is suggesting that the two schools are on the same level academically—they definitely are not—merely that the education they offer is excellent value for the cost (tuition and fees of $5,152 at Truman State; $17,586 at Cal Tech).

MONEY magazine bases its analysis primarily on data compiled with the help of Wintergreen/Orchard House of New Orleans, a publisher of college directories. Moody's Investors Service and John Minter Associates, of Boulder, Colo., supply additional information.

MONEY magazine analyzes 16 specific measures of educational quality, then compares them with each college's tuition and fees to arrive at a value rating. (For public schools, out-of-state tuitions are used to help people searching nationwide for college bargains.) In essence, the colleges that do best on the list charge lower tuitions than institutions offering an education of similar quality.

Note that the rankings include only schools whose curriculum and campus life make students of any (or no) faith feel welcome. Excluded are colleges whose main purpose is to turn out members of the clergy, colleges that require an affirmation of faith from students, colleges where the curriculum or extracurricular activities significantly reflect the ideology of a specific faith, and colleges where religious study of any nature is a significant academic requirement. In addition, we omit the service academies, highly specialized colleges, schools that require students to work during the academic year, and colleges at which more than 45 percent of the students are enrolled part-time.

Here, then, are the 16 educational factors that are analyzed to determine each college's place in the rankings:

• *Entrance examination results.* This is the percentage of freshmen who entered college with verbal and math scores above 500 on the SAT or above 23 on the composite ACT. The average percentage who did that well at all colleges: verbal 42 percent, math 60 percent on the SAT; 41 percent on the ACT.

• *Class rank.* Colleges get points for the percentage of entering freshmen who finished in either the top fifth (average: 44 percent) or the top quarter (48 percent) of their high school classes, depending on which statistic the school could supply.

• *High school grade-point average.* Using the common four-point scale, schools get points for the average high school GPA of the entering freshman class. Cal Tech and UCLA scored highest, with 3.9 vs. the average of 2.9.

• *Faculty resources.* This measure compares the number of full- and part-time undergraduates with the number of full- and part-time faculty. The lower the ratio, the more faculty attention students are likely to get. Cal Tech wins with the lowest ratio, 3 to 1, compared with the 14-to-1 national average.

• *Core faculty.* This is the ratio of students to faculty members who hold the highest degrees available in their fields. Yale is tops with a 3-to-1 ratio; the average is 15 to 1.

• *Faculty deployment.* This is the ratio of students to tenured faculty who actually teach classes. Massachusetts Institute of Technology has the best ratio, 5 to 1, far above the 34-to-1 average.

• *Library resources.* To obtain this measure, analysts divided the total of all reference materials, including books, periodicals, and microfilm, by the number of students using the campus libraries.

Higher is better: Yale's huge 1,500-to-1 ratio dwarfs the 186-to-1 average. But Harvard wins for absolute numbers: 20.3 million, handily beating runner-up Yale's 14.5 million.

• *Instructional budget.* Using U.S. Department of Education reports, analysts calculated each school's expenditure per student. Cal Tech spends the most, $39,842; the average is $5,057.

• *Student services budget.* These are the dollars a school spends on services such as career guidance and student activities. Dartmouth is the biggest spender at $4,044 per student, nearly quadruple the $1,187 average.

• *Freshmen retention rate.* This is the percentage of freshmen who return to the school the following fall. Harvard scores best with 99 percent; the average was 76 percent. A high percentage indicates that students are pleased with the education they are receiving and that the college did a good job in selecting which applicants to admit. Also, colleges that score best on this measure have the highest percentage of students who graduate within four years; 94 percent of Harvard's 1990 freshmen earned degrees in that time.

• *Four-year graduation rates.* This is the percentage of under-graduates who complete their degrees in four years. The average: 40 percent.

• *Five- and six-year graduation rates.* This is the percentage of freshmen who graduate within five (average: 53 percent) or six (average: 55 percent) years. The five-year rate is used only when colleges cannot provide the six-year rate.

• *Advanced study.* This is the percentage of each college's graduates who go on to professional or graduate schools. The average: 23 percent.

• *Default ratio on student loans.* The percentage of students who default on their loans within two years of leaving school helps identify colleges whose graduates may not be well prepared for careers. The average is 7 percent.

• *Graduates who earn doctorates.* The National Research Council counted the number of graduates from each college who went on to earn Ph.D.'s between 1983 and 1992. The University of California—Berkeley had the most: 18 percent of its graduates earned doctorates—3,640 of them—in that period.

•*Business success.* Analysts used data from *Standard & Poor's Register of Corporations, Directors and Executives,* which lists where 71,500 corporate bigwigs went to college. Yale has the most graduates in the register: 950 of them.

TOP 100

1. New College of the University of South Florida
2. Rice University (Tex.)
3. Trenton State College (N.J.)
4. Truman State University (Mo.)
5. California Institute of Technology
6. State University of N.Y. at Binghamton
7. Rutgers University—New Brunswick (N.J.)
8. University of North Carolina—Chapel Hill
9. Hanover College (Ga.)
10. Spelman College (Ga.)
11. University of Illinois—Urbana/Champaign
12. St. Mary's College of Maryland
13. University of Texas—Austin
14. State University of N.Y. at Albany
15. State University of N.Y.—College at Geneseo
16. University of Georgia

17. University of Washington
18. Fisk University (Tenn.)
19. University of Florida
20. State University of N.Y. at Stony Brook
21. Yale University (Conn.)
22. Hendrix College (Ark.)
23. James Madison University (Va.)
24. Washington and Lee University (Va.)
25. Mary Washington College (Va.)
26. Trinity University (Tex.)
27. State University of N.Y. at Buffalo
28. University of Iowa
29. Wake Forest University (N.C.)
30. Miami University (Ohio)
31. Hillsdale College (Mich.)
32. University of Wisconsin—Madison
33. Clemson University (S.C.)
34. Wabash College (Ind.)
35. University of the South (Tenn.)
36. University of Virginia
37. Emory and Henry College (Va.)
38. University of South Carolina—Columbia
39. Illinois College
40. Harvey Mudd College (Calif.)
41. Pomona College (Calif.)
42. Berry College (Ga.)
43. Johns Hopkins (Md.)
44. Harvard University (Mass.)
45. St. Bonaventure University (N.Y.)
46. New Jersey Institute of Technology
47. Creighton University (Neb.)
48. University of California—Berkeley
49. Siena College (N.Y.)
50. College of William and Mary (Va.)
51. University of Missouri—Columbia
52. Southwestern University (Tex.)

53. Grinnell College (Iowa)
54. Claremont McKenna College (Calif.)
55. Columbia University (N.Y.)
56. Dartmouth College (N.H.)
57. University of California—Los Angeles
58. Austin College (Tex.)
59. Chestnut Hill College (Pa.)
60. Virginia Polytechnic Institute
61. University of California—Davis
62. Grove City College (Pa.)
63. Georgia Institute of Technology
64. Auburn University (Ala.)
65. Florida State University
66. Texas A&M University—College Station
67. Baylor University (Tex.)
68. Centre College (Ky.)
69. Samford University (Ala.)
70. Centenary College of Louisiana
71. Swarthmore College (Pa.)
72. Rutgers University—Camden (N.J.)
73. Agnes Scott College (Ga.)
74. Drury College (Mo.)
75. Rosemont College (Pa.)
76. Princeton University (N.J.)
77. Williams College (Mass.)
78. Le Moyne College (N.Y.)
79. Birmingham–Southern College (Ala.)
80. Furman University (S.C.)
81. University of Delaware
82. Salem College (N.C.)
83. North Carolina State University
84. Transylvania College (Ky.)
85. Central College (Iowa)
86. Nazareth College of Rochester (N.Y.)
87. St. Mary's University of San Antonio (Tex.)
88. Wells College (N.Y.)

89. Bellarmine College (Ky.)
90. Stanford University (Calif.)
91. Northwestern University (Ill.)
92. Indiana University—Bloomington
93. New Mexico Institute of Mining & Technology
94. University of Kentucky
95. Sweet Briar College (Va.)
96. Ottawa University (Kans.)
97. Howard University (D.C.)
98. State University of N.Y.—College at Fredonia
99. Pennsylvania State University
100. Ohio University

Top Values Ranked by Choosiness

Here's how 45 of the top values compare when grouped with schools that are equally demanding about academic qualifications for admission. (The schools determine their own categories.)

MOST SELECTIVE

Students at these schools come from the top 20 percent of their high school classes, with average grades of B+ or better and SAT scores of at least 1,200 or ACT scores of 29 or above.

1. New College of the Univ. of South Florida
2. Rice University (Tex.)
3. California Institute of Technology
4. State University of N.Y. at Binghamton
5. University of North Carolina—Chapel Hill

6. State University of N.Y.—College at Geneseo
7. Yale University
8. Washington and Lee University (Va.)
9. Trinity University (Tex.)
10. University of Virginia
11. Harvard University (Mass.)
12. University of California—Berkeley
13. College of William and Mary (Va.)
14. University of California—Los Angeles
15. Georgia Institute of Technology

HIGHLY SELECTIVE

Students at these schools were in the top 40 percent of their high school classes, with average grades of B or better and SAT scores of 1,100 or better and ACT scores of at least 27.

1. Trenton State College (N.J.)
2. Truman State University (Mo.)
3. Rutgers University—New Brunswick (N.J.)
4. Spelman College (Ga.)
5. University of Illinois—Urbana/Champaign
6. St. Mary's College of Maryland
7. University of Texas—Austin
8. State University of N.Y at Albany
9. University of Washington
10. University of Florida
11. Hendrix College (Ark.)
12. James Madison University (Va.)
13. Wake Forest University (N.C.)
14. Florida State University
15. Texas A&M University—College Station

SELECTIVE

Students at these schools ranked in the top 50 percent of their high school classes, with average grades of B- or better and SAT scores of 950 or above and ACT scores above 22.

1. Hanover College (Ind.)
2. University of Georgia
3. University of Iowa
4. Miami University (Ohio)
5. Hillsdale College (Mich.)
6. Clemson University (S.C.)
7. Emory and Henry College (Va.)
8. University of South Carolina—Columbia
9. Berry College (Ga.)
10. St. Bonaventure University (N.Y.)
11. Creighton University (Neb.)
12. Auburn University (Ala.)
13. Birmingham–Southern College (Ala.)
14. Ottawa University (Kansas)
15. Howard University (D.C.)

Discounted Tuition

These half dozen schools offer the best values when ranked by the average amount actually paid by students, after financial aid is deducted from the official listed price for tuition and fees.

1. University of California—Berkeley
2. New College of the University of South Florida
3. State University of N.Y. at Binghamton
4. Hillsdale College (Mich.)

5. University of North Carolina—Chapel Hill
6. Grinnell College (Iowa)

Road Runners' Favorites

*These are the public schools from the top 100 list on pages 143–146
with the highest percentage of students from out of state.*

University of Delaware	58%
New College of the University of South Florida	37
Georgia Institute of Technology	37
Auburn University (Ala.)	37
University of Wisconsin—Madison	36
University of Virginia	34
College of William and Mary (Va.)	34
Truman State University (Mo.)	29
University of Iowa	29

Small but Choice

*Here are the dozen best values among schools with traditional liberal arts
programs and fewer than 1,600 students.*

1. New College of the University of South Florida
2. Hanover College (Ind.)
3. St. Mary's College of Maryland
4. Fisk University (Tenn.)

5. Hendrix College (Ark.)
6. Hillsdale College (Mich.)
7. Wabash College (Ind.)
8. Emory and Henry College (Va.)
9. Illinois College
10. Drury College (Mo.)
11. Grinnell College (Iowa)
12. Chestnut Hill College (Pa.)

SCIENTIFIC AND TECHNICAL SCHOOLS

Here are the half dozen top values among schools that specialize in science and technical programs.

1. California Institute of Technology
2. Harvey Mudd College (Calif.)
3. New Jersey Institute of Technology
4. Virginia Polytechnic Institute
5. Georgia Institute of Technology
6. North Carolina State University

Black College Buys

Among traditionally black colleges, these three represent the top values.

1. Spelman College (Ga.)
2. Fisk University (Tenn.)
3. Howard University (D. C.)

Women's Colleges

Within our "Top 100" list, these five rank highest among colleges that admit only women.

1. Spelman College (Ga.)
2. Chestnut Hill College (Pa.)
3. Agnes Scott College (Ga.)
4. Salem College (N.C.)

INDEX

153

INDEX